RASHI
ON THE TORAH
פירוש רש"י על התורה

VOLUME II

———◆———

Selected portions of
Rashi on the Torah

Annotated and
Translated
by
Rabbi Avraham Yaakov Finkel

YESHIVATH BETH MOSHE
SCRANTON, PA.

CONTENTS

———◉———

TRANSLATOR'S INTRODUCTION

This sefer is a sequel to the first volume of Rashi's midrashic commentaries on *Bereishis* and *Shemos*, offering Rashi's midrashic insights on *Vayikra, Bamidbar,* and *Devarim*.

A student of Chumash, Tanach, and Gemara, fondly thinks of Rashi as his faithful rebbi, gently guiding him along the tortuous path to understanding a mystifying verse in Chumash or an intricate *sugya* in the Gemara. No matter whether one is a young yeshivah student or an accomplished *lamdan*, one counts on Rashi's lucid and concise commentary to clarify a problematic text or uplift oneself with a poignant midrash. No one person in the past one thousand years has had such a deep impact on Jewish learning.

Rashi's commentary on the Torah offers a wonderful blend of *p'shat*—the plain meaning of verse—interspersed with a wealth of ethical and inspirational teachings of Aggadah. By including midrashic sayings in his commentary, Rashi follows the pattern of the Gemara where inspiring Aggadic teachings often are inserted into the scholarly halachic deliberations of the Sages.

The solid bond between halachah and Aggadah comes to the fore in the following midrash:

Yitzchak blessed Yaakov saying: *May G-d grant you the dew of heaven and the fat of the earth, much grain and wine* (*Bereishis* 27:28). Expounds the midrash: "Dew of heaven is Torah, fat of the earth is Mishnah, grain is halachah decrees, wine is Aggadah."

In a similar vein, the Gemara in *Chagigah* 14a compares the words of halachah to bread, and the words of Aggadah to water. Explaining this analogy, the *Menoras Hamaor* suggests: The human body requires both bread and water for survival. We usually eat bread twice a day, whereas we drink water frequently throughout the day. The soul is nourished by the bread of halachah and the water of Aggadah—halachah is necessary only when the need arises, whereas the need for Aggadah always exists.

Indeed, the Midrash says: If you want to appreciate the greatness of the Creator, study Aggadah, for through it you will get to know Him and cling to His ways (*Sifrei, Eikev* 49).

RASHI'S MAGNIFICENT TORAH COMMENTARY

Attesting to the magnificence of Rashi's commentary on the Torah, his grandson, the illustrious Tosafist Rabbeinu Tam, declared: "I also could have written a commentary on the Talmud as my grandfather did, but I'm not capable of producing a Torah commentary equal to my grandfather's work."

It is interesting to note that late in life Rashi wanted to write a new commentary, omitting the Aggadic portions, as he declared to his grandson, the Rashbam (Rabbi Shmuel ben Meir): "Had I the time, I would write another commentary based strictly on the the plain meaning of the verses" (*Rashbam* on *Bereishis* 37:2).

RASHI'S LIFE AND LEGACY

Rashi (acronym of **R**abbi **Sh**elomoh ben **Y**itzchak) was born in Troyes, France, in 1040 c.e. and died there in 1105. He traced his ancestry to the Talmudic sages Rabbi Yochanan HaSandler and Hillel HaZaken, back to David HaMelech. After receiving his early Talmudic instruction from his father, Rashi went to Mainz, Germany to broaden his knowledge under Rabbi Yaakov ben Yakar, a disciple of Rabbeinu Gershon Meor Hagolah. He then studied at the Yeshivah of Rabbi Yitzchak HaLevi in Worms. At the age of 25 he returned to his native Troyes where he founded a Yeshivah that attracted the most gifted scholars of Western Europe.

It can be said without exaggeration that Rashi has been the foremost teacher of the Jewish people for the last 900 years. He truly merits the acronym of "Rashi"—**R**abban **SH**el Yisrael, "Teacher of Yisrael."

AVRAHAM YAAKOV FINKEL
Tammuz, 5710/'10

RASHI
ON THE TORAH
פירוש רש"י על התורה

VAYIKRA
BAMIDBAR
DEVARIM

ויקרא
VAYIKRA

THE CREATION OF HEAVEN AND EARTH

1:1 And He called to Moshe, and Hashem spoke to him from the Tent of Meeting, saying.

HE CALLED TO MOSHE—[Why does the verse mention that G-d called Moshe, if it continues with, *Hashem spoke to him?*] Whenever it says, *Hashem spoke*, or, *He said*, or, *He commanded to Moshe*, He first affectionately called him [by name]. The angels, too, [lovingly] call to each other, as it says, *And one angel will call another and say, "Holy, holy, holy, Hashem . . . (Yeshayah* 6:3).

But G-d revealed Himself to the non-Jews unannounced, as it says *G-d happened upon [the heathen prophet,] Bilam (Bamidbar* 23:4), [using a term denoting] impurity.

HE CALLED TO MOSHE . . . You might think that there was an introductory call before each paragraph, to teach you otherwise the Torah says, *Hashem called Moshe and spoke to him,* teaching that Hashem only called to Moshe when He began to speak to him, but not after the [intermediate] breaks.

What purpose did these breaks serve? To give Moshe time to reflect [on the particulars] of the laws between one section and the next and between one subject and the next. [If Moshe, the greatest of all prophets, who learned from the mouth of the Almighty,

3

needed to pause and reflect on the teachings of G-d,] surely an ordinary person who is taught Torah by an ordinary teacher must pause to ponder and reflect on the subject matter at hand.

HASHEM SPOKE TO HIM . . . SAYING—G-d told Moshe: Go impress [the children of Yisrael] with these words, "It is for your sake that G-d speaks to me." Throughout the thirty-eight years that Yisrael was in the desert living under a ban because of the episode of the spies, G-d did not speak directly to Moshe, as it says, *It was at that time that all the men of war among the people finished dying. Hashem then spoke to me, saying . . . (Devarim* 2:16,17). Only after they died did G-d speak directly to me.

Another explanation for the word *saying* is: [Hashem said to Moshe,] "Go forth and tell them My commandments, bringing Me back word whether they will accept them," as it says, *Moshe brought the people's reply back to Hashem (Shemos* 19:8).

1:17 **He shall split [the bird]—with its wing feathers—without tearing it completely apart. The kohein shall then burn it on the altar, on the wood that is on the fire. It is a burnt offering, a fire offering that is a pleasing fragrance to Hashem.**

WITH ITS WING FEATHERS—The actual feathers [were burnt.] Even a commoner is sickened by the smell of burnt feathers, so why does the Torah command us to burn the feathers? [The feathers make the bird appear larger] so that the Altar can look full and beautiful even with the offering of the poor man [who can only afford a pigeon.]

[A PLEASING FRAGRANCE TO HASHEM]—It says here, *a pleasing fragrance to Hashem,* referring to a bird offering, just as it said, *a pleasing fragrance to Hashem* (1:9), concerning an animal offering. This teaches us that it does not matter to G-d whether one brings much or little, so long as one's heart is directed sincerely to Heaven.

2:1 **If a soul presents a meal offering to Hashem, his offering must consist of the best grade of meal. On it he shall pour oil and place frankincense.**

IF A SOUL PRESENTS—The only instance where the Torah mentions the word *soul* by voluntary offerings, is in the case of the meal offering. Usually only the poor man brings an [inexpensive] meal offering. The Holy One, blessed be He, said, "I regard [his meal offering] as if he had offered his soul."

5:17,18 If a person sins by violating one of all the negative commandments of Hashem, and he has no definite knowledge, he bears responsibility. He must bring a ram . . .

WITHOUT DEFINITE KNOWLEDGE, HE STILL BEARS RESPONSIBILITY. HE MUST BRING . . . This section concerns one who does not know whether or not he violated a prohibition that is punishable by *kareis* (excision, premature death). For example, a piece of forbidden animal fat and a piece of permissible animal fat were placed before him. Thinking that both were permissible fats, he ate one piece. He was then told, "One of these pieces was forbidden fat," obligating him to bring a "guilt-offering because of doubt", which protects him [from punishment], as long as he does not find out that he actually sinned. If he later finds out that in fact he sinned, he brings a sin offering.

Rabbi Yose HaGelili says: The Torah punishes someone who does not know whether or not he sinned; surely the Torah will punish someone who knows that he sinned.

Rabbi Yose says: You can learn from Adam Harishon the reward in store for the righteous. Adam was given only one negative commandment, and he transgressed it. Look how many deaths were decreed on him and his descendants! Which measure of G-d is greater, that of reward or that of punishment? Certainly that of reward. If so many deaths were decreed against him and his descendants through the measure of punishment which is less [than the measure of reward,] you can calculate the great measure of reward for one who refrains from eating forbidden foods, like *piggul*,[1] or

---

[1] A sacrifice that became invalid because of the kohen's improper intentions at the time of bringing the offering

nosar,[2] or he fasts on Yom Kippur. He will surely earn merit for himself, his descendants and his descendants' descendants, until the end of all generations.

Rabbi Akiva says: It says, *On the testimony of two witnesses or three witnesses . . . (Devarim* 17:6). Since testimony can be established through two witnesses, why does the Torah also specify *or three witnesses?* To include the third one to be strict with him and place him on equal footing with the other two witnesses regarding the punishment of false testimony. If the Torah punishes an accessory with the same severity as one who commits a sin, how much more so will the Torah reward an accessory to one who fulfills a mitzvah on the same level as one who fulfills a mitzvah!

Rabbi Elazar ben Azaria says: It says, *When you reap your grain harvest and forget a sheaf in the field, you must not go back to get it . . . so that Hashem your G-d will bless you (Devarim* 24:19). Thus the Torah bestows blessing on someone who [forgot his sheaf and] performed a mitzvah without his being aware of it. By the same token, if someone had a *sela* coin wrapped in the seam of his garment, and it falls out and is found by a poor man who buys food with it, the Holy One, blessed be He, will bestow blessing on the one [who lost the coin].

2:21 [This is the law] if a person sins and breaks faith against Hashem by lying to his neighbor regarding a pledge or a loan or a robbery, or by defrauding his neighbor.

IF A PERSON SINS—Rabbi Akiva says: What is the Torah teaching us when it says, *he breaks faith against Hashem?* Whoever lends and borrows, or buys and sells, does so only before witnesses and with a document. Therefore, if he denies such a claim, he contradicts the witnesses and the document. However, when someone deposits an article with his neighbor, he does not want anyone to know about it, except [G-d], the Third Party between them. Therefore, when he denies it, he breaks faith with [G-d, who is] the Third Party between them.

---

2   A portion of a sacrifice left over after the prescribed time

צו

TZAV

———◆———

6:1 Command to Aharon and his descendants: This is the law of the burnt offering: The burnt offering shall remain on the altar's hearth all night until morning, so that the fires of the altar can be ignited with it.

COMMAND TO AHARON AND HIS DESCENDANTS—The word *command* always denotes urging [to fulfill a mitzvah promptly and meticulously] for the present and for future generations. Rabbi Shimon says: The Torah particularly needs to urge people to fulfill mitzvos where monetary loss is involved [as in the case of the burnt offering when an expensive animal is totally consumed.]

6:4 He shall remove his garments and put on other garments. He shall then take out the ashes to a clean place outside the camp.

HE SHALL REMOVE HIS GARMENTS—Rather than an obligation, this is a rule of proper practice, so he should not soil the garments in which he officiates, while taking out the ashes. [An analogy:] A servant should not serve his master a glass of wine wearing the clothes he wore while cooking for his master. Therefore, [the verse continues,] *and put on other garments,* [meaning inferior garments,] for they are inferior to the garments [he wore while conducting the service].

SHEMINI

⟞≡◉≡⟝

THE DEATH OF AHARON'S SONS

10:3 Moshe said to Aharon, "This is what Hashem meant when He said, 'I will be sanctified through those close to Me, and I will be glorified before the entire people.'" Aharon remained silent.

I WILL BE GLORIFIED BEFORE THE ENTIRE PEOPLE—When the Holy One, blessed be He, exacts judgment on the righteous, He becomes feared, exalted, and praised. If this is so in regard to the righteous, surely this is so in regard to the wicked. In the same vein, it says, *You are awesome, O G-d, from Your sanctuaries* (*Tehillim* 68:36). Do not read from *Your sanctuaries*; read instead, "because of Your sanctified ones."

10:6 Moshe said to Aharon and his sons, "Do not go without a haircut and do not tear your garments, otherwise you will die, bringing divine wrath upon the entire community. Your brothers, the entire family of Yisrael, shall mourn for the ones whom Hashem burned.

YOUR BROTHERS, THE ENTIRE FAMILY OF YISRAEL, SHALL MOURN—From here we learn that when Torah scholars are afflicted, all of Yisrael is required to mourn for them.

KOSHER ANIMALS

11:1,2 Hashem spoke to Moshe and Aharon telling them to speak to the children of Yisrael and say to them: These are the living creatures that you may eat, from all the animals in the world.

THESE ARE THE LIVING CREATURES—The Torah uses the term living creatures [rather than *animals*] because Yisrael is bound to G-d and worthy of being spiritually alive. Therefore He separated them from ritual uncleanliness and decreed mitzvos on them, but He did not forbid anything to the nations.

A parable: A physician visited an incurably sick person and allowed him to eat anything he wished, but when he visited a patient who would recover, he prescribed a strict diet to ensure that he would live. The same applies to the nations of the world and Yisrael, as cited in Midrash Tanchuma.

11:43 Do not make yourself disgusting [by eating] any creature that creeps. Do not defile yourselves with them and become contaminated through them.

AND BECOME CONTAMINATED THROUGH THEM—If you defile yourselves [by eating] these creatures on earth, I too, will defile you in the World to Come and in the Heavenly Academy.

11:44 For I am Hashem your G-d, and you shall sanctify yourselves and become holy, since I am holy. And you shall not defile your souls [by eating] creatures that creep on the land.

FOR I AM HASHEM YOUR G-D—Just as I am holy, for I am Hashem, your G-d, so too, you must make yourselves holy by sanctifying yourselves on earth.

AND BECOME HOLY—For I will make you holy above and in the World to Come.

תזריע
TAZRIA

———◆◆◆———

13:46 As long as he has the *tzaraas*[3] mark, it shall defile him and he will be unclean. He must remain alone, and his place shall be outside the camp.

HE MUST REMAIN ALONE—so other unclean people [who are not stricken with *tzaraas*] will not be near him. The Rabbis said: Why is he singled out from other unclean persons to remain alone? Just as he separated a husband from his wife and a man from his friend through his slanderous speech, so shall he be isolated.

14:4 The kohein shall order to be taken for the one undergoing purification, two live kosher birds, a piece of cedar, some crimson thread, and a hyssop branch.

KOSHER BIRDS . . . Since these afflictions result from the sin of *lashon hara* (slander and tale-bearing) which is caused by chattering, the purification of the *metzora* necessitates birds which chatter endlessly with twittering sounds.

A PIECE OF CEDAR—[Wood of a tall tree was selected] because these [*tzaraas*] afflictions are a [punishment] for haughtiness [which is the root cause of *lashon hara*].

---

3   A type of leprously which makes one ritually unclean.

SOME CRIMSON THREAD, AND A HYSSOP BRANCH—[The Hebrew word for thread, is *tolaas,* which also translates as a worm.] How can he be healed [from his *tzaraas* affliction]? Instead of being haughty [like the cedar], he should lower himself like a worm and a [lowly] hyssop.

14:34 When you come to the land of Canaan, which I am giving to you as an inheritance, I will place the *tzaraas* affliction in a house in the land you inherit.

I WILL PLACE THE TZARAAS AFFLICTION—This is a good tiding for them. The houses will be stricken with *tzaraas,* because the Amorites hid treasures of gold in the walls of their houses throughout the forty years that Yisrael were in the desert. Because of the *tzaraas,* the [Jewish] owner would tear down the house, finding the treasure.

14:35 The owner of the house shall come and tell the Kohein, "It appears to me as if there is something like an affliction in the house."

THERE IS SOMETHING LIKE AN AFFLICTION IN THE HOUSE—Even a Torah scholar who is certain that it is a *tzaraas* affliction, should not definitively declare, "There is an affliction in the house." Rather he should say, "There is something like an affliction in the house."

אחרי מות
ACHAREI MOS

16:1 Hashem spoke to Moshe after the death of Aharon's two sons, who died when they brought an [unauthorized] offering before Hashem.

HASHEM SPOKE TO MOSHE AFTER THE DEATH OF AHARON'S TWO SONS—What do the words [*after the death of Aharon's two sons*] come to teach us? Rabbi Eliezer ben Azariah explains with a parable about two doctors who visited a patient. The first doctor told him, "Do not eat cold food, nor lie down in a cold, damp place." The second doctor advised him, "Do not eat cold food, nor lie down in a cold damp place, otherwise you will die the way so-and-so died." The second doctor's warning is more forceful than the first doctor's warning. The phrase, *after the death of Aharon's two sons*, [is a forceful warning to Aharon: Heed the message of the following verse and refrain from entering the inner Sanctuary at all times, otherwise you will die as your two sons died].

THE ATONEMENT PROCESS OF YOM KIPPUR

16:16 And he will make atonement on the sacred for the defilements of B'nei Yisrael, as well as for their rebellious acts and all their inadvertent misdeeds. He shall then perform [exactly] the same [ritual] in the Tent of Meeting

which remains with [B'nei Yisrael] even when they are unclean.

WHICH REMAINS WITH [B'NEI YISRAEL] EVEN WHEN THEY ARE UN-
CLEAN—Although they are unclean, the *Shechinah* is among them.

18:28 But [you shall not cause] the land to vomit you out
when you defile it, as it vomited out the nation that
was there before you.

BUT [YOU SHALL NOT CAUSE] THE LAND TO VOMIT YOU OUT—This
can be compared to a prince who was fed loathsome food which he
could not stomach, and vomited it out. Likewise, Eretz Yisrael cannot bear transgressors [and spews them out]. The Targum translates: "The Land empties itself [of the transgressors.]"

19:2 Speak to the entire community of B'nei Yisrael and say to them, "You must be holy, for I, Hashem, your G-d, is holy."

YOU MUST BE HOLY—Separate yourselves from sexual immorality and from transgression, for wherever you find restraint against sexual immorality, you find holiness. [For example: It says,] *[The kohanim] shall not marry an immoral or profaned woman*, followed by . . . *for I, Hashem, am making you holy* (*Vayikra* 21:8).

19:14 Do not curse the deaf. Do not place a stumbling block before the blind. You must fear your G-d, I am Hashem.

DO NOT PLACE A STUMBLING BLOCK BEFORE THE BLIND.—Before anyone who is "blind" regarding the matter at hand. Do not give someone advice that is unsuitable for him. [For example:] Do not say to someone: "Sell your field and buy a donkey [with the proceeds,]" if you are deluding him in order to buy [the field] from him.

YOU MUST FEAR YOUR G-D—Since others can not know if his intention was for good or evil, and he can evade [the charge of evil intent] by saying, "My intent was for the best," it says, *You must fear your G-d*—the One who knows your thoughts. Similarly, regarding every matter which is secreted in the heart of the one who does it, [and] others cannot know [his real intent], it says, *You must fear your G-d.*

19:15 Do not pervert justice. Do not give special consideration to the poor, nor show respect to the great. Judge your fellow fairly.

JUDGE YOUR FELLOW FAIRLY—Another interpretation: Judge your fellow favorably, [always giving him the benefit of the doubt.]

19:18 Do not take revenge, nor bear a grudge against the children of your people. You must love your neighbor as you love yourself. I am Hashem.

DO NOT TAKE REVENGE—[For example:] A person asks his neighbor, "Lend me your sickle," and the neighbor replies, "No!" The next day, the latter says to him, "Lend me your ax." If he says to him, "I will not lend it to you, just as you did not lend to me," this constitutes revenge. And what constitutes "bearing a grudge"? If he says to him, "You are welcome to it. I am not like you, who did not lend to me." This constitutes bearing a grudge, for he keeps the hatred in his heart, although he does not take revenge.

YOU MUST LOVE YOUR NEIGHBOR AS YOU LOVE YOURSELF—Rabbi Akiva says: This is a fundamental principle of the Torah.

19:35 Do not commit a perversion of justice, in measures of length, weight, or volume.

DO NOT COMMIT A PERVERSION OF JUSTICE—This verse is not dealing with litigation, for the Torah has already said, *Do not pervert justice* (19:15). So what is the *justice* that is repeated here? It refers to [just conduct in dealing with] measures, weights, and liquid measures. This teaches us that one who measures [something in commerce] is called a judge, and if he falsifies the measure, he is considered as one who perverts justice. [Accordingly, like a corrupt judge,] he is called perverse, hated, loathsome, banned, and an abomination. [Furthermore,] he brings about the five things that a corrupt judge causes: (1) he defiles the land; (2) he desecrates the name of G-d; (3) he drives away the *Shechinah*; (4) he causes Yisrael to fall by the sword; (5) and he causes Yisrael to be exiled from their Land.

19:36 You must have an honest balance, honest weights, an honest dry measure, and an honest liquid measure. I am Hashem your G-d who took you out of Egypt.

WHO TOOK YOU OUT OF EGYPT—on condition [that you observe these commandments.]

Another explanation: [G-d says,] "In Egypt I distinguished between the drop [of semen that led to the birth] of a firstborn and the drop [of semen that did not lead to the birth] of a firstborn. [So, too] I am faithful to exact punishment on one who secretly dips his weights in salt [to increase their weight] thereby cheating [the seller] who does not notice [that they have been manipulated]."

20:3 I will direct My anger against that person and cut him off [spiritually] from among his people, since he has given his children to Molech, thus defiling that which is holy to Me and profaning My holy name.

THUS DEFILING THAT WHICH IS HOLY TO ME—[This does not refer to the Sanctuary, rather to] the congregation of Yisrael which is sanctified to Me.

20:15 If a man performs a sexual act with an animal he must be put to death, and the animal shall likewise be killed.

AND THE ANIMAL SHALL LIKEWISE BE KILLED—Though the man sinned, what sin did the animal commit? Since sin occurred through [the animal], the Torah says, "Let it be stoned." We can draw a logical conclusion from this; if a human being who can distinguish between good and evil, brings evil upon his fellow [causing him to transgress, he will surely be punished].

In a similar vein, it says, *Destroy, utterly destroy, all the places where the nations whom you are driving out worship their gods* (*Devarim* 12:2). We can draw a logical inference: If the Torah says about trees, when they cause man to sin, "Destroy them! Burn them! Obliterate them!" though they can neither hear nor see, surely a man who leads his fellow astray from the path of life to the path of death is blameworthy.

20:26 You shall be holy to Me, for I, Hashem, am holy, and I have separated you from among the nations to be Mine.

AND I HAVE SEPARATED YOU FROM AMONG THE NATIONS TO BE MINE—If you are separated from them [through your observance of the mitzvos] you are Mine, but if not, you will belong to Nevuchadnetzar and his cohorts and be exiled from the holy land.

Rabbi Elazar ben Azariah says: How do we know that one should not say, "I find pork repulsive," or, "I do not want to wear a garment made of a mixture of wool and linen," but rather he should say, "I really wish to, but my Father in Heaven has forbidden it, what can I do?" Because the Torah says, *I have separated you from among the nations to be Mine.* Your separation from them must be for the sake of My Name, separating yourself from transgression and accepting upon yourself the yoke of the Kingdom of Heaven.

אמור

EMOR

22:32 Do not desecrate My holy name, rather I should be sanctified among B'nei Yisrael. I am Hashem, Who makes you holy.

DO NOT DESECRATE MY HOLY NAME—by transgressing My words intentionally. Since it says, *Do not desecrate*, what is added by the words, *I should be sanctified*? [The verse means to] give your life [in martyrdom] in order to sanctify My name. Perhaps [one must offer his life] even when he is alone? [To teach you otherwise] it says, *among B'nei Yisrael*—[in the presence of ten Jews.] And when one offers his life, he should do so expecting to die for his love of G-d, for if someone offers his life expecting a miracle [to save him from death], G-d will not perform the miracle for him. Thus Chananiah, Mishael, and Azariah, did not offer their lives expecting [to be saved by] a miracle [when the wicked Nevuchadnetzar cast them into a fiery furnace, for refusing to bow down to the statue,] as it says, *Behold, our G-d whom we worship is able to save us. He will rescue us from the fiery, burning furnace and from your hand, O king. But if [He does] not, let it be known to you, O king, that we will not worship your god, and we will not prostrate ourselves to the golden statue that you have set up* (Daniel 3:17,18). [Since they did not rely on a miracle, G-d saved them].

23:22 When you reap your land's harvest, do not completely harvest the ends of your fields. Nor shall you gather individual stalks that have fallen. You must leave them for the poor and the stranger. I am Hashem, your G-d.

WHEN YOU REAP . . . R. Avdimi b. R. Yosef said: Why is this [agricultural prohibition] placed amid the festival laws with Pesach and Shavuos on one side and Rosh Hashanah, Yom Kippur, and Sukkos on the other side? To teach you that whoever properly gives gleanings, the forgotten sheaves, and the corner of the field to the poor, is regarded as though he built the Beis Hamikdash and brought his offerings in it.

24:3 Aharon shall light the lamp consistently with this oil. [It shall burn] from evening to morning, outside the curtain partition of the testimony in the Tent of Meeting. This shall be an eternal law for all generations.

OUTSIDE THE CURTAIN PARTITION OF THE TESTIMONY—[The partition] was located in front of the Ark which is called "Testimony" [because it contained the Tablets of Testimony.] However our Rabbis expounded that *the Testimony* alludes to the lamp on the far left side [of the Menorah], which was a testimony to all people on earth that the *Shechinah* rests on Yisrael, for it held the same amount of oil as the other [six] lamps, yet [although the Kohein] began kindling from it, [it still burned the next morning] while he finished [cleaning the other lamps that had burned out,] and it continued to burn.

24:22 There shall be one law for you, for both the convert and the native born, for I am Hashem, your G-d.

I AM HASHEM, YOUR G-D—I am the G-d for all of you. Just as I attach the Oneness of My Name to you, so do I attach the Oneness of My Name to converts.

בהר
BEHAR

————◦❁◦————

25:14 When you buy or sell [land] to your neighbor, do not cheat one another.

WHEN YOU BUY OR SELL [LAND] TO YOUR NEIGHBOR . . . The verse can also be expounded [in this manner:] How do we know that one who wishes to sell [a parcel of land] should sell it to his fellow Jew? It says, *When you sell [land], sell it to your neighbor.* And how do we know that if one wishes to buy [something], he should buy it from his fellow Jew? It says, *or when you buy from your neighbor.*

25:17 Do not wrong one another. You shall fear your G-d, since I am Hashem, your G-d.

DO NOT WRONG ONE ANOTHER—Here the Torah warns against annoying someone with words. One may not anger his fellow [Jew]. Neither may one give bad advice to benefit his own life-style. One might think, "Who knows whether I had evil intentions?" Therefore it says, *You shall fear your G-d*—Who knows man's thoughts. About all thoughts secreted in the heart, known only to the person thinking them, it says, *You shall fear your G-d.*

25:18 And you shall keep My decrees and safeguard My laws and do them, and you will live securely in the land.

AND YOU WILL LIVE SECURELY IN THE LAND—[The preceding chapter deals with the laws of *shemittah*—the sabbatical year. We learn from this verse that] for the sin of [neglecting] *shemittah*, Yisrael will be exiled [from their land], as it says [in reference to the exile,] *the land will be appeased regarding its Sabbaths. The land will rest and enjoy its sabbatical rest* (*Vayikra* 26:25). The seventy years of the Babylonian exile correspond to the seventy *shemittah* years that Yisrael did not observe.

25:35 When your brother becomes impoverished and his hand falters in the community, you must come to his aid. Help him survive, whether he is a convert or a native Jew.

YOU MUST COME TO HIS AID—Do not allow him to decline and fall completely, so that it becomes difficult to raise him [to his previous position.] Instead, strengthen him as soon as he begins to falter. This can be compared to a burden on a donkey. As long as the burden is still on the donkey [even if it begins to slip,] it can be kept in place by one person; but once it falls to the ground, even five people cannot raise it.

25:38 I am Hashem your G-d, who brought you out of Egypt to give you the land of Canaan, to be a G-d to you.

WHO BROUGHT YOU OUT—And [there] I distinguished between a firstborn and one who was not firstborn. So too, I know and will inflict punishment on one who lends money to a Jew with interest, claiming that the money belongs to a non-Jew.

Another interpretation: *I brought you out of Egypt* in order that you accept My mitzvos upon yourselves, even when it will be difficult for you.

[TO GIVE YOU THE LAND OF CANAAN,] TO BE A G-D TO YOU—I am a G-d for whoever lives in Eretz Yisrael, but whoever leaves [Eretz Yisrael], it is as if he worships idols.

25:46 They, [the non-Jewish slaves,] are hereditary property that you shall pass down to your children, and you shall thus have them serve you forever. However, where your fellow Jews are concerned, you must not dominate one another to break one's spirit.

YOU MUST NOT DOMINATE ONE ANOTHER—[The prohibition is repeated here] to include a leader who dominates his people and a king who tyrannizes his attendants.

26:1 Do not make yourselves false gods. Do not set up a stone idol or a sacred pillar for yourselves. Do not place a stone pavement in your land so that you can prostrate yourselves on it, for I am Hashem your G-d.

DO NOT MAKE YOURSELVES FALSE GODS—This is addressed to one who was sold [as a slave] to a non-Jew. He may not say, "Since my master has illicit relations, I will do likewise. Since my master worships idols, I will do likewise. Since my master desecrates the Shabbos, I will do the same." Therefore these verses are stated here. Furthermore, the passages [from the beginning of Chapter twenty-five until the end of *Behar*] are written in chronological order: At first one is warned regarding *shemittah* [the seventh year]. If he coveted money and disregarded the laws of *shemittah,* [he will lose his money] and ultimately sell his movables; therefore [the laws of *shemittah,*] are followed by, *When you sell to your neighbor or buy from the hand of your neighbor,* (25:14). This verse [refers to movable goods, because it] speaks of something acquired from hand to hand. If he does not repent he will eventually be forced to sell his inheritance (25:25). If he still does not repent, he will eventually sell his home, and, if he continues unrepentant, he will have to borrow money with interest (25:35-38). The latter punishments are harsher than the earlier ones. Accordingly, if he still does not repent, he will eventually have to sell himself [to his fellow Jew as a servant] (25:35-46). Finally, if he still has not repented, not only will he have to sell himself to his fellow Jew, he will be forced to sell himself to a non-Jew.

בחקתי
BECHUKOSAI

———◦◉◦———

26:3 If you follow My laws and are careful to keep My commandments.

IF YOU FOLLOW MY LAWS—You might think this refers to the fulfillment of the mitzvos. However [the second clause], *and are careful to keep My commandments*, already connotes the fulfillment of the mitzvos. So what is the meaning of, *If you follow My laws?* It means one should toil in the study of Torah.

AND ARE CAREFUL TO KEEP MY COMMANDMENTS—One should toil in the study of Torah in order to observe and fulfill the mitzvos, as it says, *Learn them and safeguard them, so that you will be able to keep them* (*Devarim* 5:1).

26:6 I will grant peace in the land so that you will sleep without fear. I will rid the land of dangerous animals, and the sword will not pass through your land.

I WILL GRANT PEACE IN THE LAND—You might say, "We have food and drink, but without peace there is nothing." That is why after all these blessings it says, *I will grant peace in the land*. From here we learn that peace is equal to all [blessings]. Indeed we say [in the *Shacharis* prayer]: *Blessed are You, Hashem Who makes peace and creates everything.*

26:8 Five of you will be able to chase away a hundred, and a hundred of you will defeat ten thousand, and your enemies will fall before your sword.

FIVE OF YOU WILL BE ABLE TO CHASE AWAY A HUNDRED, AND A HUNDRED OF YOU WILL DEFEAT TEN THOUSAND—But is this the correct proportion? [Following the ratio of five to one hundred,] it should have said one hundred of you will defeat two thousand. Thus [the Torah teaches us that] there is no comparison between a few who fulfill the Torah and many who fulfill the Torah.

26:9 I will turn to you, making you fertile and numerous, thus keeping My covenant with you.

I WILL TURN TO YOU—I will turn away from all My concerns to pay your reward. A parable: A king had a group of workers; most worked minimally, except for one laborer who worked a great deal. When they presented themselves to be paid, the king quickly paid them all a small amount. However to the tireless worker he said, "They only worked a minimal amount, but now I must pay attention to figure out the substantial amount I owe you." Similarly, G-d will quickly pay the nations the small amount He owes them for their few good deeds, and then He will focus His attention on the Jewish people to calculate their great reward.

THUS KEEPING MY COVENANT WITH YOU—a new covenant; not like the first covenant which you broke, but a new covenant which will not be broken, as it says, *I will seal a new covenant with the House of Yisrael and the House of Yehudah; not like the covenant I sealed with their forefathers . . . which they abrogated* (*Yirmeyah* 31:31,32).

26:12 I will walk among you. Thus I will be a G-d to you, and you will be a nation [dedicated] to Me.

I WILL WALK AMONG YOU—I will walk with you in Gan Eden as one of you, and you will not be terrified of Me. You might think that you will not fear Me [since I am so close to you], therefore the Torah says, *I will be a G-d to you.*

26:13 I am Hashem your G-d, Who brought you out from Egypt from your enslavement to them. I broke the bands of your yoke, and I led you with your heads held high.

I AM HASHEM YOUR G-D—I deserve that you believe Me that I can do all these things, for *I brought you out from Egypt* and performed great miracles for you.

THE CHAPTER OF ADMONITION

26:19 I will break the pride of your strength; and I will make your skies like iron and your land like copper.

I WILL BREAK THE PRIDE OF YOUR STRENGTH—This is the Beis Hamikdash, as it says, *Behold, I am profaning My Sanctuary, the pride of your strength* (*Yechezkel* 24:21).

26:32 I will desolate the land so that your enemies who live there will be astonished.

I WILL DESOLATE THE LAND—This is a good measure for Yisrael, for Yisrael's enemies will not find the Land worthwhile [to occupy], and it will remain uninhabited.

26:33 I will scatter you among the nations and keep the sword drawn against you. Your land will remain desolate, and your cities in ruin.

I WILL SCATTER YOU AMONG THE NATIONS—This is a harsh decree, for when the population of a country is exiled to one location, they derive comfort from one another by seeing each other. But Yisrael was scattered as by a winnowing shovel, for when winnowing barley, one grain does not cling to the next.

26:37 They will fall over one another as if [chased] by the sword, although no one is pursuing. You will not have the wherewithal to stand up before your foes.

THEY WILL FALL OVER ONE ANOTHER AS IF [CHASED] BY THE SWORD—. . . The Midrash says: *They will fall over one another* means: One person will fall because of someone else's sin, since all Jews are responsible for one another.

26:41 [It was for this] that I will also remain indifferent to them and I will bring them into their enemies' land. But when the time finally comes that their stubborn heart is humbled, I will forgive their sin.

AND I WILL BRING THEM INTO THEIR ENEMIES' LAND—I Myself will bring them [into exile]. This is a good thing for Yisrael, for if they say, "Since we were exiled among the nations, we may as well behave like them." [G-d will say,] "I will not allow them to do so, rather, I will install My prophets to bring them back under My wings," as it says, *As for what enters your minds—it shall not be! As for what you say, "We will be like the nations, like the families of the lands, to worship wood and stone," as I live, the word of Hashem Elokim—I swear that I will rule over you with a strong hand and an outstretched arm and with outpoured wrath* (Yechezkel 20:32,33), [causing you to do teshuvah.]

26:42 I will remember My covenant with Yaakov as well as My covenant with Yitzchak, as I will remember My covenant with Avraham, and I will remember the land.

I WILL REMEMBER MY COVENANT WITH YAAKOV—In five places is Tanach the name Yaakov is written in full [with a *vav*], and in five places in Tanach the name Eliyahu is written without a *vav*. [This is because] Yaakov took the letter *vav* from the name Eliyahu as a security that [the prophet] will come to announce the redemption of [Yaakov's] children.

I WILL REMEMBER MY COVENANT WITH YAAKOV—Why are the Patriarchs mentioned in reverse order? To let you know that [the redemption can come to pass] in the sole merit of Yaakov, the youngest. But if that is not enough, then Yitzchak's merit is together with his. And if even that is not enough, Avraham whose merit is certainly sufficient is also with them.

Why is the expression "remembering" not mentioned regarding Yitzchak? [Because Yitzchak does not need to remembered, for G-d says,] "The ashes of Yitzchak, [who was brought on the altar to become a burnt offering,] are constantly visible in front of My eyes, gathered up and lying on the Altar."

26:46 These are the decrees, laws, and codes that Hashem set between Himself and B'nei Yisrael at Mount Sinai through the hand of Moshe.

THE CODES—[The plural implies] two codes, the Written Torah and the Oral Torah. This teaches us that both were given to Moshe on Mount Sinai.

27:7 For a person over sixty years old, [or over] the endowment valuation shall be fifteen shekels for a man, and ten shekels for a woman.

FOR A PERSON OVER SIXTY YEARS OLD—At an advanced age, a woman's valuation becomes closer to that of a man. Thus the valuation of a man in his old age decreases by more than two thirds, [going from fifty shekels to fifteen], while the valuation of a woman [in her old age] decreases by exactly two thirds, [falling from thirty to ten shekels]. This proves the saying: An old man in the house means discomfort in the house; an old woman in the house is a treasure in the house.

במדבר

Bamidbar

——◆——

1:1 Hashem spoke to Moshe, in the Sinai Desert, in the Tent of Meeting, on the first day in the second month in the second year of the Exodus, saying: Count the heads of the congregation of Yisrael. . .

HASHEM SPOKE TO MOSHE IN THE SINAI DESERT . . . Because G-d loves [B'nei Yisrael] He counts them frequently. When they left Egypt He counted them (*Shemos* 12:37), and when they perished in the wake of the sin of the golden calf, He counted them to see how many survived (*Shemos* 32:28). [And now, shortly after the erection of the *Mishkan,*] when His Shechinah came to dwell among them, He counted them. For on the first day of Nissan the *Mishkan* was erected, and on the first day of Iyar, He counted them.

1:49 Do not take a tally or a census of the Levi'im together with B'nei Yisrael.

DO NOT TAKE A TALLY OR A CENSUS OF THE LEVI'IM—Because the [Levi'im, the] legion of the King, deserve to be counted separately. Another explanation: The Holy One, blessed be He, foresaw that all those counted from twenty years and over would be sentenced to die in the desert [for rebelling in the episode of the spies]. Therefore he said, "Do not let these [Levi'im] be included

28

[in the death sentence,] for they belong to Me, since they did not err by bowing to the [golden] calf."

3:1 These are the descendants of Aharon and Moshe on the day that Hashem spoke to Moshe on Mount Sinai.

THESE ARE THE DESCENDANTS OF AHARON AND MOSHE— Although only the sons of Aharon are mentioned, they are considered descendants of Moshe, because he taught them Torah. This teaches us that if one teaches his friend's son Torah, Scripture considers it as if he had fathered him.

ON THE DAY THAT HASHEM SPOKE TO MOSHE—They became his offspring when he taught them what he had learned from G-d.

3:38 Camping in the east, in front of the Mishkan, shall be Moshe and Aharon and his sons, who keep the charge of the Sanctuary as a trust for B'nei Yisrael. Any unauthorized person who approaches shall die.

MOSHE AND AHARON AND HIS SONS—Near the division under the flag of Yehudah[4], which included the tribes of Yissachar and Zevulun. [Good neighbors] are good for the righteous, and good for his neighbor. Since [these three tribes, Yehudah, Yissachar, and Zevulun] were neighbors of Moshe who was immersed in Torah study, they became great Torah scholars, as it says, *Yehudah is my lawgiver* (*Tehillim* 60:9). About the descendants of Yissachar it says, *they had understanding of the times* (1 *Divrei Hayamim* 12:33), and it says, *two hundred [of Yissachar] were heads of the Sanhedrin.* From Zevulun came *those who wield the scribe's quill* (*Shofetim* 5:14).

4　The tribes of Yehudah, Yissachar and Zevulun camped in the east.

נ ש א

NASO

———◆◇◆———

5:10 The sacred offerings of each individual remain his own property. When a man gives to the kohein he will have.

THE SACRED OFFERINGS OF EACH INDIVIDUAL REMAIN HIS OWN—
. . . An Aggadic interpretation of, *The sacred offerings of each individual remain his own* is: If one withholds his tithes, not giving them [to the kohein and the Levi], those tithes shall become his [only income], for eventually his field will produce only a tenth of its usual crop.

WHEN A MAN GIVES TO THE KOHEIN HE WILL HAVE.—When a man gives to the kohein the gifts he is entitled to, he, [the donor,] will acquire great wealth.

5:12 Speak to B'nei Yisrael and say to them: Any man whose wife is suspected of committing adultery and being false to her husband.

ANY MAN WHOSE WIFE IS SUSPECTED OF COMMITTING ADULTERY AND BEING FALSE TO HER HUSBAND—What is written before this subject? *The sacred offerings of each individual remain his own.* If one withholds the gifts of the kohanim, be assured that he will be forced to come to [the kohein] with his unfaithful wife.

ANY MAN WHOSE WIFE—[The Hebrew for *Any Man* is written *a man, a man*. The double expression] teaches that [the suspected adulteress] has been unfaithful both to G-d, who is called *the Man of War* (*Shemos* 15:3) above, and to her husband, who is *her man* in this world.

ANY MAN WHOSE WIFE IS SUSPECTED OF COMMITTING ADULTERY— Our Sages taught: People do not commit adultery unless they are seized by a spirit of foolishness, [for the Hebrew word for adultery used here is, *sisteh*, which has the same root as, *shotah* – a fool.] And so it says, *He who commits adultery with a woman is devoid of sense* (*Mishlei* 6:32).

6:2 Speak to B'nei Yisrael and say to them: [This is the law] when a man or woman sets himself apart by expressing a nazirite vow of abstinence for the sake of Hashem.

WHEN A MAN OR WOMAN SETS HIMSELF APART—Why does the chapter dealing with the *nazir* follow the chapter of the suspected adulterous woman? To tell us that whoever sees an adulterous woman in her disgrace, should vow to abstain from wine, for [wine] bring to adultery.

7:1 On the day that Moshe finished erecting the Mishkan, he anointed it and sanctified it along with all its vessels. He also anointed the altar and all its utensils.

ON THE DAY THAT MOSHE FINISHED [*KALLOS*] ERECTING THE MISHKAN—[The Hebrew word for "finished" is *kelos*, however,] here it is written *kallos*, which means "bride," to tell us that on the day the Mishkan was set up, Yisrael was like a bride entering the *chuppah*.

בְּהַעֲלֹתְךָ
BEHA'ALOSECHA

8:2 Speak to Aharon and say to him, "When you light the lamps, the seven lamps shall illuminate the face of the Menorah."

WHEN YOU LIGHT—Why is the chapter of the Menorah placed immediately after the chapter of the [offerings of] the leaders?

When Aharon saw the dedication offerings of the leaders he was dismayed, since neither he nor his tribe joined them in the dedication. The Holy One, blessed be He, said to him, "By your life! Yours is greater than theirs. For you [and your descendants] will light and clean the lamps [forever]."

8:19 I have given the Levi'im as a gift from B'nei Yisrael to Aharon and his descendants. They shall [henceforth] perform the service for B'nei Yisrael in the Mishkan and atone for B'nei Yisrael. B'nei Yisrael will then not be afflicted with plague when B'nei Yisrael approach the Sanctuary.

I HAVE GIVEN . . . *B'nei Yisrael* is mentioned five times in this verse, demonstrating the love G-d has for them. Their name is repeated as many [as five] times in one verse, to correspond to the five books of the Torah.

8:24 This is [the rule] regarding the Levi'im. Beginning at the age of twenty five they shall participate in the work force engaged in service of the Mishkan.

BEGINNING AT THE AGE OF TWENTY FIVE—But in another verse it says, *From the age of thirty* (4:3)! How can this be reconciled? At the age of twenty five they come to learn the laws of the service. They study for five years, and at the age of thirty they begin performing the service. This teaches us that a student who has not been successful in his learning for five years will never achieve mastery.

9:7 "We are ritually unclean because of contact with the dead," the men said [to Moshe]. "Why should we lose out and not be able to bring the offering of Hashem at the right time, along with the rest of B'nei Yisrael?"

WHY SHOULD WE LOSE OUT—[A group of people were ineligible to bring their pesach offering because they were ritually unclean. Moshe] said to them, "Holy things cannot be offered by a person in a state of uncleanness."

They countered, "[We understand that an unclean person may not eat the *korban pesach*,] but let the blood [of our *korban pesach*] be sprinkled [on the Altar on our behalf] by a clean kohein, and let the flesh be eaten when we are clean.

Moshe said to them, "Wait, while I listen what Hashem will command regarding you." Moshe spoke like a student who relies on hearing the answer [to his question] from his teacher. Fortunate is the man who is confident that he can speak with the *Shechinah* whenever he wishes.

This chapter should have been said through Moshe, as is the rest of the Torah, [rather than on the initiative of others]. But these [sincere people] gained the merit of having [this chapter] said through them, because good things are brought about by good men.

10:34 Hashem's cloud remained over them by day when they travelled from the camp.

HASHEM'S CLOUD REMAINED OVER THEM—Seven clouds are mentioned in connection with their travels: four were in the four directions, one above, one below, and one in front of them which leveled the elevations, raised the hollows, and killed snakes and scorpions.

10:35 When the Ark went forth Moshe said, "Arise Hashem, and scatter Your enemies! Let those that hate You flee before You!"

THOSE THAT HATE YOU—These are those that hate Yisrael, for whoever hates Yisrael hates G-d, as it says, *Those who hate You have raised their heads* (*Tehillim* 83:3). [And the following verse explains] who they are, *They plot deviously against Your people* (ibid. 83:4).

MOSHE PLEADS ON BEHALF OF YISRAEL

11:15 If You are going to do this to me, do me a favor and kill me! Don't let me see myself getting into such a terrible predicament!

IF YOU ARE GOING TO DO THIS TO ME—[The Hebrew text for the word *You* used here is *At* which is the feminine form, hinting] that Moshe became weak like a woman when G-d showed him the punishment He planned to bring on [Yisrael]. Therefore he said to G-d, "Kill me first."

11:16 Hashem said to Moshe, "Assemble for Me seventy of Yisrael's elders—the ones you know to be the people's elders and leaders. Bring them to the Tent of Meeting, and let them stand there with you.

ASSEMBLE FOR ME SEVENTY OF YISRAEL'S ELDERS—[Moshe is now told to assemble a group of elders.] What happened to the first group of elders, who had officiated back in Egypt? As it says, *Go and gather the elders of Yisrael* [and announce that Hashem will deliver B'nei Yisrael from slavery and bring them out of Egypt] (*Shemos* 3:16). [The original elders] died in the fire of Tav'eirah (11:3). In fact, they deserved [to die earlier,] at Sinai, [but their lives were spared,] as it says, *Hashem did not unleash His power against the leaders of Yisrael, [who had acted disrespectfully,] for while they were having a vision of G-d, they ate and drank* (*Shemos* 24:11). They behaved irreverently, like someone chewing bread while speaking to the king, as implied by, *they ate and drank*. However, G-d did not want to cause mourning at the Giving of the Torah, so he punished them [in the fire of Tav'eirah].

THE ONES YOU KNOW TO BE THE PEOPLE'S ELDERS AND LEADERS— The ones you know as the foremen over the Jews in Egypt during their rigorous labor. [The foremen,] having mercy on [their fellow Jews], were flogged because [the Jews could not produce their daily quota of bricks], as it says, *The foremen of B'nei Yisrael were flogged* (*Shemos* 5:14). Just as they suffered in Yisrael's distress, let them be appointed as their elders, now that Yisrael has attained greatness.

BRING THEM TO THE TENT OF MEETING—Persuade them with words, "How fortunate are you to be appointed leaders over the children of G-d!"

AND LET THEM STAND THERE WITH YOU—So B'nei Yisrael seeing this, will treat them with esteem and respect, saying, "How beloved are these who have entered [the Tent of Meeting] with Moshe to hear the speech from the mouth of the Holy One, blessed be He."

11:17 When I will come down and speak with you there, I will cause some of the spirit that you possess to emanate, and I will grant it to them. They will share with you the responsibility for the people. You will then not have to bear the responsibility all alone.

I WILL GRANT IT TO THEM—At that moment Moshe could be compared to a candle on a candlestick. Everyone lights from it, yet its brightness is not diminished.

THEY WILL SHARE WITH YOU THE RESPONSIBILITY FOR THE PEOPLE—Make it clear to them [that they will become elders] provided they take upon themselves the burden of My children who are unruly and rebellious.

11:22 Even if all the sheep and cattle were slaughtered, could there be enough [meat] for them? If all the fish in the sea were caught, would it be sufficient?[5]

EVEN IF ALL THE SHEEP AND CATTLE WERE SLAUGHTERED—This is one of the four verses that Rabbi Akiva and Rabbi Shimon expound differently. Rabbi Akiva says: *600,000 men on foot, and You are saying that You will give them enough meat to eat for a full month?* (11:21). The verse is to be taken literally; [Moshe was asking if it were possible for G-d to provide sufficient meat for them.] Where did Moshe seem to display a greater lack of faith in G-d? Here, or [at the Waters of Merivah] when he said, *Listen now you rebels!* (20:10)? [Surely, this case is worse. If so, why was Moshe punished for the incident of Merivah, but not for this graver offense?] Since in the present case, Moshe only expressed his doubt to G-d privately, G-d spared him not punishing him, whereas in the case of Merivah because he spoke in public, G-d did not spare him.

Rabbi Shimon says: G-d forbid! This never entered the mind of [Moshe,] that tzaddik, [to doubt that G-d could provide enough meat for 600,000 men.] Would the one about whom it says, *He is trusted throughout My house* suggest that G-d cannot provide for us

---

5   In response to the request of the nation that they be provided with meat, Hashem told Moshe that he would give them all meat for thirty days.

sufficiently? Rather, this is what he meant: [B'nei Yisrael are] *600,000 men on foot, and You are saying that You will give them enough meat to eat for a full month,* and afterwards you will kill such a great nation [for murmuring against You]? Will sheep and cattle be slaughtered for them, and then they will be killed with this meat satisfying them forever? Will You be praised for this? Do people say to a donkey, "Eat this *kor*-measure of barley, and then we will cut off your head?"

G-d answered, "If I do not give them [meat,] they will say My power is limited. Would you rather they think G-d's power is limited? Let them and a hundred like them perish, as long as My power is not limited in their eyes for even one moment."

12:1 **Miriam and Aharon began speaking against Moshe because of the Kushite woman he had married. For the woman that [Moshe] had married was indeed a Kushite.**

MIRIAM AND AHARON BEGAN SPEAKING AGAINST MOSHE— [Miriam] spoke first, therefore the verse mentions her first. How did she know Moshe had separated from his wife? Rabbi Nassan says: Miriam was standing next to Tzipporah when Moshe was told that Eldad and Meidad were prophesying in the camp. When Tzipporah heard this she said, "Woe to these wives if their husbands became prophets, for they will separate from their wives just as my husband separated from me." This was the source of Miriam's information which she repeated to Aharon. If Miriam who did not mean to slight Moshe was punished, surely one who [intentionally] slights his fellow [will be punished].

12:4 **Hashem suddenly said to Moshe, Aharon, and Miriam, "All three of you, go out to the Tent of Meeting." All three went out.**

SUDDENLY—[G-d] suddenly revealed Himself to [Miriam and Aharon], when they were unclean because they had relations with their spouses. They [needed water to purify themselves and] cried out, "Water, water!" [G-d] thereby showed them that Moshe had acted correctly by separating from his wife, since the *Shechinah* regularly revealed itself to him, and there was no set time when G-d would speak to him.

12:8 With him I speak face to face, in a vision not containing allegory, so that he sees a true picture of G-d. How can you not be afraid to speak against My servant, against Moshe.

AGAINST MY SERVANT, AGAINST MOSHE—The Torah does not say, "Against My servant Moshe," but, *against My servant, against Moshe.* [Hashem complained to them for speaking] *against My servant*—even if he were not Moshe. And *against Moshe* – for even if he were not My servant, it would be fitting to fear him. And all the more so, since he is My servant, and the servant of the king is like the king himself. You should have said, "The King does not love him for nothing." Should you reply [that he is unworthy of My love and] I am unaware of his actions, that statement is worse than the previous one.

12:9 Hashem's anger flared against them, and He left.

HASHEM'S ANGER FLARED AGAINST THEM, AND HE LEFT.—After informing them of their reprehensible behavior He [left,] placing them under a ban. All the more so, a human being should not express his anger at someone before telling him of his grievance.

12:10 The cloud moved from above the tent and Miriam was afflicted with tzaraas, white like snow.

THE CLOUD MOVED FROM ABOVE THE TENT—and only then *Miriam was afflicted with tzaraas*. This may be compared to a king who said to [his son's] teacher, "Punish my son, but not until I leave, as I pity him."

12:13 Moshe cried out to Hashem, "O G-d, please heal her!"

O G-D, PLEASE HEAL HER!—The Torah is teaching proper conduct: If one asks a favor from his friend, he should precede his request with two or three words of supplication, and only then should he make his request.

PLEASE HEAL HER—Why didn't Moshe say a drawn out prayer? So Yisrael should not say, "His sister is in distress, yet he stands and prays at length."

Another interpretation: So Yisrael should not say, "For his sister he prays at length, but for our sake he does not prolong his prayers.

12:15 For seven days Miriam remained quarantined outside the camp, and the people did not move on until Miriam returned home.

THE PEOPLE DID NOT MOVE ON—This honor was accorded to her by G-d because of the short time she stayed with Moshe when he was cast into the Nile, as it says, *[Moshe's] sister stood herself at a distance to see what would happen to him* (*Shemos* 2:4).

שלח לך
SHELACH LECHA

———◆◉◆———

13:2 Send out men for yourself to explore the Land of Canaan that I am about to give to B'nei Yisrael.

SEND OUT MEN FOR YOURSELF—Why does the chapter of the spies follow the chapter dealing with Miriam's [punishment]? Because she was punished for malicious slander, when she criticized her brother; and the wicked spies did not learn their lesson [and slandered Eretz Yisrael].

13:22 They went up through the Negev, and he came to Chevron, and there were Achiman, Sheishai, and Talmai, descendants of the Giant. Chevron had been built seven years before Tzo'an in Egypt.

HE CAME TO CHEVRON—[It does not say, "and they came to Chevron," in the plural] because Calev went there by himself to prostrate himself on the graves of the Patriarchs, [praying] that he not be enticed by the conspiracy of his comrades. Therefore it says, *I will give Calev the land he walked* (*Devarim* 1:36), and it says, *They gave Chevron to Calev* (*Shofetim* 1:20).

CHEVRON HAD BEEN BUILT SEVEN YEARS BEFORE TZO'AN IN EGYPT—Is it possible that Cham built Chevron for Canaan, his youngest son, before building Tzo'an in Egypt for his eldest son?

[The meaning of the verse is] that [Chevron] was seven times more fertile than Tzo'an, and produced the finest crops, letting us know how superior Eretz Yisrael is. Chevron is the rockiest part of Eretz Yisrael, and was therefore chosen as a burial place. Egypt is the best country in the world, as it says, *It was like Hashem's own garden, like the land of Egypt* (*Bereishis* 13:10). Tzo'an is the best part of Egypt, for it is the residence of the kings, as it says, *For his princes were in Tzo'an* (*Yeshayah* 30:4). Yet Chevron was seven times better than Tzo'an, [which proves the excellence of Chevron and Eretz Yisrael].

13:25 At the end of forty days they returned from exploring the land.

AT THE END OF FORTY DAYS THEY RETURNED FROM EXPLORING THE LAND—Doesn't Eretz Yisrael measure 400 parsa by 400 parsa, and an average person walks ten parsa per day? Thus, it takes forty days to walk from east to west, yet they traversed both its length and its width [in forty days]! Since the Holy One, blessed be He, knew that He would sentence them with a year [of wandering in the desert] for every day [they spent exploring the Land], he shortened the way [so they covered both the length and the width of the Land in forty days].

13:30 Calev tried to quiet the people for Moshe. "We must go up and occupy the land," he said. "We can do it!"

WE MUST GO UP—even to Heaven, and even if He tells us to build ladders and go up there. We will succeed at whatever He says.

14:18 Hashem is slow to anger, great in love, and forgiving of sin and rebellion. He does not clear those who do not repent, but keeps in mind the sins of the fathers for their children, grandchildren, and great-grandchildren.

HASHEM IS SLOW TO ANGER—at the righteous and at the wicked. When Moshe ascended on high, he found the Holy One, blessed be He, sitting and writing the words, "Hashem is slow to anger."

Moshe asked Him, "At the righteous?"

The Holy One, blessed be He, replied, "Even at the wicked."

[Moshe] responded, "Let the wicked perish!"

G-d replied, "By your life! You will need this thing."

When B'nei Yisrael sinned with the golden calf and the spies, Moshe prayed to Him saying, "Slow to anger."

Said the Holy One, blessed be He, "But you said to Me, '[Only] to the righteous.'"

Moshe retorted, "But You said to me, 'Even to the wicked.'"

14:37 The men who had given a bad report about the land thus died before Hashem in a plague.

THUS DIED BEFORE HASHEM IN A PLAGUE—By the death that they deserved, [by a punishment that was] measure for measure. They sinned with the tongue [by slandering Eretz Yisrael], so their tongues lengthened until [they reached] their navels, and maggots came from their tongues and entered their navels. That is why it says, in "the" plague before Hashem, and not in "a" plague. This is implied by the phrase *before Hashem*. [They received] the plague that befit them according to the attributes of the Holy One, blessed be He, who metes out punishment measure for measure.

15:39 This shall be to you as *tzitzis*, and when you see them you shall remember all of Hashem's commandments so as to keep them. You will then not stray after your heart and your eyes, which have led you to immorality.

YOU SHALL REMEMBER ALL OF HASHEM'S COMMANDMENTS—The numeric value of the word *tzitzis* is 600 (90+10+90+10+400). Add to that the eight threads and five knots, and you have a total of 613 [which is the number of the mitzvos in the Torah].

YOU WILL THEN NOT STRAY—The heart and the eyes are the spies for the body, brokering for it the sins [desired by its animal nature.] The eye sees, the heart covets, and the body commits the transgression.

15:41 I am Hashem your G-d who brought you out of Egypt to be your G-d. I am Hashem your G-d.

I AM HASHEM YOUR G-D—Why is this phrase repeated? So Yisrael should not say, "Why did G-d say [we should do the mitzvos]? Is it not to perform them and receive reward? We would rather not perform them and we will do without the reward." Therefore, Hashem says, "I am your King, whether you like it or not." In the same vein it says, *Surely with a strong hand will I reign over you* (*Yechezkel* 20:33).

Another explanation: Why is the exodus mentioned [in this verse? To tell you:] It was I who distinguished between the drop [of semen] of an [Egyptian] firstborn and a drop that was not of a firstborn. So too, in the future I will discern and punish those who attach *tzitzis* dyed with indigo [a substance derived from a plant] to their garments, claiming that it is [the Torah-prescribed] *techeiles* [which is extracted from a *chilazon* mollusk].

I quote the following from the work of R. Moshe Hadarshan: Why does the chapter of the wood gatherer [who desecrated the Shabbos] follow the chapter about idolatry? To teach that one who desecrates the Shabbos is regarded as though he worshipped idols. For the mitzvah of keeping Shabbos—just like the prohibition against idolatry—is equivalent to all the mitzvos of the Torah put together. And so it says, *You descended on Mount Sinai . . . and You gave [Your people] righteous laws and true teachings . . . You made known Your sacred Shabbos to them* (*Nechemiah* 9:13.14), [showing that Shabbos is on par with all the mitzvos]. Likewise, the mitzvah of tzitzis [follows that of the one who desecrates Shabbos, because the mitzvah of *tzitzis*] is equivalent to all the mitzvos, as it says [in the portion of *tzitzis*,] *You will thus remember and keep all My mitzvos* (15:40).

ON THE CORNERS OF THEIR GARMENTS—[On the four corners,] corresponds to the four expressions of redemption that were said in Egypt: *I will take you out . . . I will save you . . . I will redeem you . . . I will take you* (*Shemos* 6:6,7).

A THREAD OF SKY-BLUE WOOL—This refers to the death of the Egyptian firstborn, [because the Hebrew for sky-blue wool is, *techeiles* similar to] the Aramaic word *shikul* which means loss. Furthermore: The plague struck the Egyptians at night, and the color of *techeiles* is similar to that of the sky which turns black at dusk. Its eight threads represent the eight days Yisrael waited from when they left Egypt until they sang the Song at the Sea.

קרח

KORACH

KORACH'S REBELLION

16:1 And Korach the son of Yitzhar, the son of Kehos, the son of Levi took himself [to begin a rebellion,] along with Dasan and Aviram the sons of Eliav, and On the son of Peles, descendants of Reuven.

THE SON OF YITZHAR, THE SON OF KEHOS, THE SON OF LEVI—[The verse] does not add [that Levi was the son of Yaakov], because Yaakov prayed that his name be omitted from this quarrel, as it says, *Let my soul not enter their plot* (*Bereishis* 49:6). However his name is mentioned in connection with Korach, when his genealogy is traced for the service of the Levi'im on the platform [in the Beis Hamikdash], as it says, *Son of Korach, son of Yitzhar, son of Kehos, son of Levi, son of Yisrael* (1 *Divrei Hayamim* 6:22.23).

DASAN AND AVIRAM—Since the tribe of Reuven was settled in the south, neighbors to Kehos and his children who also camped in the south, they joined with Korach in the rebellion. Woe to the wicked, and woe to his neighbor!

16:4 When Moshe heard this [rebellious talk] he threw himself on his face.

HE THREW HIMSELF ON HIS FACE . . . Since this was already [B'nei Yisrael's] fourth failing. When they sinned with the calf, *Moshe pleaded* (*Shemos* 11:2); By the episode of the complainers, *Moshe prayed* (*Bamidbar* 11:2); In connection with the spies, *Moshe said to Hashem, "And what will happen when the Egyptians will hear about it"* (14:13); but with Korach's rebellion, he became discouraged. This may be compared to a prince who misbehaved against his father. His friend appeased the king, once, twice, and three times, however when the prince defied [the king] a fourth time, the friend became discouraged, saying, "How much can I bother the king? Perhaps he will no longer accept my pleading!"

16:5 And he spoke to Korach and his whole party, saying, "In the morning Hashem [will show that He] knows who is His and who is holy, and He will bring them close to Him. He shall choose who [shall be allowed to] bring offerings to Him."

"IN THE MORNING HASHEM [WILL SHOW THAT HE] KNOWS WHO IS HIS—According to the Midrashic interpretation, Moshe said, *in the morning*, [rather than, "tomorrow"] implying, "G-d marked His universe with boundaries. Can morning be turned into evening? [Surely not!] So too, you cannot cancel [Aharon's appointment as Kohein Gadol], for just as it says [in reference to the creation of the world,] *It was evening and it was morning . . . and He separated* (*Bereishis* 1:5.6), so too, [it says about the appointment of Aharon,] *Aharon was set apart to sanctify him* (1 *Divrei Hayamim* 23:13)."

16:6 This is what you must do. Let Korach and his entire party take fire pans.

THIS IS WHAT YOU MUST DO—What prompted [Moshe] to say this to them? He told them: Idol worshippers have multiple forms of worship and many priests, and they do not all assemble in the same temple. [However,] we have only one G-d, one Ark, one Torah, one Altar, and one Kohein Gadol, yet all 250 of you want to become Kohein Gadol. I also desire to do so. Now I am offering that you perform the service G-d cherishes more than any other—the [burning of] the incense which is more valuable than any other offering. However it contains a deadly poison which burned Nadav and Avihu [when they brought unauthorized incense]. Therefore, [Moshe] warned them, *The man whom Hashem chooses shall be the holy one* (16:7), meaning, G-d has already chosen the holy one. Don't we know that the one chosen will be the holy one? Moshe told [Korach and his party,] "I am emphasizing this, so you should not be punished, for only the one chosen by G-d will survive, and the rest will perish."

16:7 Place fire in them and offer incense on them before Hashem, tomorrow. The man whom Hashem chooses shall be the holy one. You sons of Levi have gone too far.

YOU SONS OF LEVI HAVE GONE TOO FAR—[Moshe said,] I have told you something of great significance, [stressing that the course you are embarking on is perilous.] Weren't they fools to offer the incense after being warned by Moshe? They sinned mortally, as it says, *The fire pans belonging to the men who committed a mortal sin* (17:3). What prompted Korach, an intelligent person, to do such a foolish thing? His vision led him astray. He [prophetically] saw a chain of important people descending from him, including Shemuel who was equal in importance to Moshe and Aharon. [Korach] said, "For his sake I will be spared." [He also saw] twenty-four watches of Levi'im [performing services in the Beis Hamikdash,] descendants of his grandsons, all prophesying through *ruach hakodesh*, as it says, *All these were the sons of Heiman* (1 *Divrei Hayamim* 25:5). He said, "Is it possible that all this greatness should emanate from me, and I should remain silent?" Therefore when Moshe said, *The man whom Hashem chooses shall be the holy one,* Korach assumed Moshe meant that everyone else would perish but the one to survive referred to himself. However, he did not see correctly, for his sons did *teshuvah* [and did not die]. Moshe, however, foresaw correctly.

16:12 Moshe then sent word to Dasan and Aviram, the sons of Eliav. "We won't come," was their response.

MOSHE THEN SENT WORD—From here we learn that one should not prolong a quarrel [for Moshe took the first step towards reconciliation]. Moshe sought them out to win them over with peace talks.

16:15 Moshe became very angry. He prayed to Hashem, "Do not accept their offering. I did not take a single donkey from them, nor did I harm any of them."

DO NOT ACCEPT THEIR OFFERING—According to its simple meaning, [Moshe prayed,] "Do not accept the incense they will offer to You tomorrow." According to the Midrash [Moshe prayed,] "I know they have a share in the daily communal offerings. Please do not accept their portions favorably. Let the fire [on the Altar] avoid it, not consuming it."

16:27 [The people] withdrew from around the dwelling of Korach, Dasan, and Aviram. And Dasan and Aviram went out standing defiantly at the entrance of their tents, along with their wives, sons, and infants.

ALONG WITH THEIR WIVES, SONS, AND INFANTS—Come and see how dreadful quarreling is. The earthly court punishes [an accused] only after he reaches puberty, and the heavenly court does not punish until one reaches the age of twenty, but here even nursing babies were punished.

17:13 [Aharon] stood between the dead and the living, and the plague was checked.

[AHARON] STOOD BETWEEN THE DEAD AND THE LIVING—He grabbed the angel, forcibly holding him.

The angel said to him, "Allow me to accomplish my mission."

Aharon answered, "Moshe ordered me to stop you."

[Replied the angel,] "I am G-d's messenger, and you are only Moshe's messenger."

[Aharon] replied, 'Moshe does not say anything on his own; [he speaks] only by order of the Al-mighty. If you do not believe me, the Holy One, blessed be He, and Moshe are at the entrance of the Tent of Meeting. Come with me and ask them. This is the meaning of the statement, *Aharon returned to Moshe* (17:15).

Another interpretation: Why [did Moshe tell Aharon to stop the plague] through incense? Because Yisrael slandered and maligned the incense, saying it was a deadly poison, since it caused the death of Nadav and Avihu, and through it 250 people were burned. The Holy One, blessed be He said, "You shall see that it stops plague; it is only sin that causes death."

חקת
CHUKAS

———◦◎◦———

19:2 This is the Torah's decree as commanded by Hashem. Speak to B'nei Yisrael and have them bring you a perfect red cow which has no blemish and which has never borne a yoke.

THIS IS THE TORAH'S DECREE—Satan and the nations of the world taunt Yisrael, saying, "What is [the meaning of] this commandment, and what purpose does it serve?" Therefore the Torah refers to this commandment as a decree, [as if to say,] "It is a decree before Me; you have no right to question [its rationale]."

THE FOLLOWING COMMENTARIES ARE CULLED FROM MIDRASH RABBI MOSHE HADARSHAN

19:3,5,6,9 Give it to Elazar the kohein, and he shall have it brought outside the camp. It shall then be slaughtered in his presence. The cow shall then be burned in [Elazar's] presence. Its skin, flesh, blood, and entrails must be burned. The kohein shall take a piece of cedar wood, some hyssop, and some crimson wool, and throw them into the burning cow. A ritually clean person shall gather up the cow's ashes and place them outside the camp in a clean place. They shall be a keepsake for the community of B'nei

50

Yisrael to be used for the sprinkling water as a means of purification.

ATONEMENT FOR THE GOLDEN CALF

HAVE THEM BRING YOU—[The red cow] must [be bought] with the personal funds of the people. Just as they removed their golden nose rings [to fashion] the [golden] calf, so shall they use their own money to bring [the red cow] as an atonement.

A RED COW—This may be compared to a slave woman's son who sullied the king's palace, whereupon the order was given, "Let the mother come and clean her son's mess." So too, "Let the [red] cow come to atone for the [sin of the golden] calf."

RED—This brings to mind the verse, *If your sins are like scarlet red they will become white as snow* (*Yeshayah* 1:13).

PERFECT—Because B'nei Yisrael who were perfect became flawed [through the sin of the golden calf]; let this red cow atone for them, restoring their former perfection.

WHICH HAS NEVER BORNE A YOKE—This atones for their sin of throwing off the yoke of [obedience] to G-d.

TO ELAZAR THE KOHEIN—Just as [the people] gathered around Aharon who was a kohein, [demanding that] he make the golden calf, [so too,] the atonement shall be made by a Kohein. Since Aharon made the calf, he did not perform the service [of the red cow], for an accuser, [Aharon, who made the golden calf,] cannot act as a defender.

THE COW SHALL THEN BE BURNED—Just as the [golden] calf was burned.

A PIECE OF CEDAR WOOD, SOME HYSSOP, AND SOME CRIMSON WOOL—These three objects correspond to the three thousand men who were killed in the aftermath of the episode of the golden calf.

The cedar is the tallest tree, and the hyssop is the lowest herb, indicating that when a haughty person sins out of arrogance, he will be forgiven if he humbles himself like the hyssop and the lowly worm.

THEY SHALL BE A KEEPSAKE—Just as the sin of the golden calf is laid away for punishment for future generations, as it says, *on the day that I make My account I will take this sin of theirs into account* (*Shemos* 32:34), [so are the ashes of the red cow held in storage as a token of forgiveness]. And just as the golden calf defiled all those who were involved with it, so does the red cow cause those involved in its preparation to become ritually unclean. And just as the people were cleansed through the fine powder [into which Moshe ground the golden calf], as it says, *He scattered [the fine powder] on the water* (ibid. 32:20), so too, *Some of the dust [of the red cow] . . . shall be placed in a vessel [that has been filled with water directly] from a running spring* (*Bamidbar* 19:17).

20:1 In the first month, the entire community of B'nei Yisrael came to the Tzin Desert, and the people stopped in Kadesh. Miriam died there and was buried.

MIRIAM DIED THERE—Why does the chapter of Miriam's death follow immediately after the chapter of the red cow? To tell you that just as an offering brings atonement, so does the death of the righteous bring atonement.

MIRIAM DIED THERE—She died through a kiss [from G-d's mouth, rather than by the angel of death]. Why doesn't it mention [explicitly that she died] "by Hashem's mouth"? Because it is not respectful to mention this about G-d [regarding a woman.] However, in connection with Aharon's [death] it says, *He died by Hashem's mouth* (33:38), as it says about Moshe's death (*Devarim* 34:5).

20:2 The people did not have water and they began demonstrating against Moshe and Aharon.

THE PEOPLE DID NOT HAVE WATER—From here [we learn] that it was in Miriam's merit that they had the spring [in the desert] for forty years.

PUNISHMENT OF MOSHE AND AHARON

20:12 Hashem said to Moshe and Aharon, "You did not have enough faith in Me to sanctify Me in the presence of B'nei Yisrael! Therefore, you shall not bring this assembly to the land that I have given them."[6]

YOU DID NOT HAVE ENOUGH FAITH IN ME—The Torah reveals [Moshe and Aharon's sin to let us know] that were it not for this one sin [of striking the rock] they would have entered the Land. Thus people will not say, "Moshe and Aharon committed the same sin as the generation of the desert about whom it was decreed that they will not enter [Eretz Yisrael]."

[Elsewhere Moshe asked,] *Even if all the cattle and sheep were slaughtered, could there be enough [meat] for them* (11:22)? Wasn't this a more grievous sin than [striking the rock instead of speaking to it]? Since [Moshe's question] was asked in private, the Torah spares him, [not punishing him], however, here, [where he struck the rock] in the presence of all Yisrael, the Torah does not spare him in order to sanctify G-d's name.

TO SANCTIFY ME IN THE PRESENCE OF B'NEI YISRAEL—Had you spoken to the rock and it had given forth [water], I would have been sanctified in the eyes of the community. They would have

---

6   Hashem commanded Moshe to speak to the rock and it would give forth water. Moshe hit the rock instead and was punished.

said, "If this rock, which neither hears nor speaks and does not need sustenance, fulfills the word of G-d, all the more should we.

20:13 These are the Waters of Dispute where B'nei Yisrael disputed with Hashem, and where He was [nevertheless] sanctified.

HE WAS [NEVERTHELESS] SANCTIFIED—For Moshe and Aharon died because of [the Waters of Dispute]. When G-d judges His holy ones, He is feared and sanctified by the people. And so it says, *You are awesome, O G-d, because of Your holy ones* (*Tehillim* 68:36), and, *I will be sanctified through those close to Me* (*Vayikra* 19:3).

20:14,15 Moshe sent messengers from Kadesh to the king of Edom. "So says your brother Yisrael, you know all the travails that have beset us. Our fathers went down to Egypt and we lived in Egypt many years. The Egyptians mistreated both us and our fathers."

BOTH US AND OUR FATHERS—From here we learn that our fathers agonize in the grave when Yisrael suffers punishment.

20:16 We cried out to Hashem and He heard our voice and sent an angel and took us out of Egypt.

HE HEARD OUR VOICE—Through the blessing given to us by our Father [Yitzchak], *The voice is the voice of Yaakov* (*Bereishis* 27:22), which guarantees that when we cry out we will be answered.

AN ANGEL—meaning Moshe. From here [we learn] that the prophets are called angels. Similarly it says, *They mocked the angels of Hashem* (2 *Divrei Hayamim* 36:16) [meaning, the prophets].

20:17 Please, let us pass through your land. We will not go through fields or vineyards, and we will not drink spring water. We will travel along the king's highway, not turning aside to the right or to the left, until we pass through your territories.

WE WILL NOT DRINK SPRING WATER—He should have said, "water from your wells." Moshe actually said the following, "Although we have manna to eat and our own spring to drink from, we will not drink from it, but we will buy food and drink from you, for your benefit." From here we learn that although a guest may have his own food, he should buy [his meals] from the owner of the inn, in order to benefit his host.

20:18 Edom responded, "Do not pass through my land lest I greet you with the sword!"

LEST I GREET YOU WITH THE SWORD!—You boast about "the voice" you inherited from your father [Yaakov,] declaring, *When we cried out to Hashem, He heard our voice* (20:16). We will greet you with the sword our father [Eisav] bequeathed to us, [for Yitzchak blessed Eisav,] *You shall live by the sword* (*Bereishis* 27:40).

AHARON'S DEATH

20:23 Hashem said to Moshe and Aharon at the Hor Mountain on the border of the land of Edom, saying.

ON THE BORDER OF THE LAND OF EDOM—This teaches that because [Yisrael] became close to the wicked Eisav, their work came to a halt, and they lost this righteous [Aharon]. Similarly, the prophet said to Yehoshafat, *When you joined up with Achaziahu, Hashem brought your accomplishments to a halt* (2 *Divrei Hayamim* 20:37).

20:26 Divest Aharon of his vestments and place them on his son Elazar. Aharon will then be gathered up [to his ancestors] and die there.

HIS VESTMENTS . . . [Moshe said to Aharon], "Enter the cave." He
entered. Moshe saw a bed made ready and a candle burning,
whereupon he said, "Go up on the bed." He went up. "Extend
your hands." He extended them. "Close your mouth." He closed
it. "Shut your eyes." He shut them. At that moment Moshe wished
to die such a death. Therefore he was told [prior to his death],
Prepare to die just as your brother Aharon died (*Devarim* 32:50).

20:29 The people realized that Aharon had died. The entire family of Yisrael mourned Aharon for thirty
days.

THE PEOPLE REALIZED THAT AHARON HAD DIED—When they saw
Moshe and Elazar descended without Aharon, they asked, "Where
is Aharon?"

[Moshe] told them, "Aharon died."

They replied, "Is it possible that [Aharon,] the one who defied
the angel [of death] stopping the plague, can be overpowered by
the angel of death?" Thereupon Moshe asked for mercy, and the
ministering angels showed them [Aharon] lying on the bed. Seeing
him, they believed.

THE ENTIRE FAMILY OF YISRAEL—Both the men and women, for
Aharon had pursued peace, promoting love between feuding par-
ties and between man and wife.

21:6 Hashem sent the poisonous snakes against the people;[7] they bit the people and a large number of B'nei
Yisrael died.

THEY BIT THE PEOPLE—Let the snake which was punished for slander, punish those who maligned [the manna]. Let the snake for

---

7   The people complained about the fact that they were in the desert where nothing grew and that they had to subsist on the Manna.

which all types of food taste the same, punish those thankless people for whom one thing [the manna] changes into a variety of tastes.

21:7 The people came to Moshe and said, "We have sinned by speaking against G-d and you. Pray to Hashem to remove the snakes from us." Moshe prayed for the people.

MOSHE PRAYED FOR THE PEOPLE—From this we learn that someone who is asked forgiveness should not be heartless, refusing to forgive.

21:8 Hashem said to Moshe, "Make for yourself [the image of] a venomous snake and place it on a pole. Everyone who is bitten shall look at it and live."

EVERYONE WHO IS BITTEN SHALL LOOK AT IT AND LIVE—Our Rabbis said: Did the [image of the] snake kill, or did the [image of the] snake keep alive? The Torah is explaining that when Yisrael looked upward, subjugating their hearts to their Father in Heaven, they were healed, but otherwise they perished.

21:14,15,16 It is therefore told in the Book of Hashem's Wars, "What He gave at the Sea of Reeds and the streams of Arnon." And the spilling of the streams that turned to settle at Ar and leaned toward the border of Moav. From there to the spring. This is the well regarding which Hashem said to Moshe, "Gather the people, and I will give them water!"

IT IS THEREFORE TOLD—Concerning this encampment and the miracles that happened there.

IN THE BOOK OF HASHEM'S WARS—When they relate the miracles that happened to our forefathers, they will relate, *What He gave at the Sea of Reeds and the streams of Arnon.* Just as we relate the mir-

acles of the Red Sea, so too, we should recount the miracles that
happened at the stream of Arnon, for there, too, many great miracles were performed.

What were those miracles?

AND THE SPILLING OF THE STREAMS—The blood of the Amorites
who were hidden there was spilled there.

[Wandering through the wilderness, B'nei Yisrael had to pass
through a gorge between two mountains.] The mountains were
high and the gorge was deep and narrow. The mountains were so
close to each other that a man standing on one mountain could
speak to his fellow standing on the opposite mountain. The road
passed through the gorge.

The Amorites said, "When Yisrael enters the land by passing
through this gorge, we will come out of the caves in the mountains
above them and kill them [by shooting] arrows and slinging stones
at them." There were clefts in the rocks on the Moabite side [of the
gorge], and there were protrusions [jutting out] like horns and
breasts directly opposite those clefts on the mountain on the
Amorite side.

When B'nei Yisrael prepared to pass through, the mountain [on
the Amorite side which later would become part of] Eretz Yisrael,
trembled like a maidservant going out to greet her mistress, and
moved toward the mountain on the Moabite side. Then the protrusions joined the clefts, killing the Amorites [lying in ambush
there]. This is the meaning of, *that turned to settle at Ar*. Since the
mountain swung from its place, moving to the side of the Moabite
border and attaching itself to it, *it leaned toward the border of Moav*.

FROM THERE TO THE SPRING—From there the flow [of the dead
Amorites blood] came to the well. How so? The Holy One, blessed
be He, said, "Who will inform B'nei Yisrael of these miracles?" As
the saying goes, "If you give bread to a child, let his mother know
[and make her aware of the kindness]."

After they passed through, the mountains returned to their

places, and the well [that accompanied B'nei Yisrael on their wanderings] brought up the blood of the slain, together with their arms and limbs carrying them around the camp. Seeing this, B'nei Yisrael [realized the great miracle G-d had performed and] intoned a song.

THE SONG OF THE SPRING

21:18 A spring excavated by princes, dug by the leaders of the people, through the lawgiver's staff. And from the desert to Matanah.

A SPRING . . . DUG BY THE LEADERS OF THE PEOPLE, THROUGH THE LAWGIVER'S STAFF—On Moshe's orders, for Moshe was called the lawgiver, as it says [concerning Moshe], *for there the portion of the lawgiver is hidden* (*Devarim* 33:21). Why isn't Moshe mentioned in this song [about the spring]? Because he was punished on account of the spring; and since Moshe's name is not mentioned, the name of the Holy One, blessed be He, is not mentioned either. A parable: A king was invited to a banquet. He said, "If my friend is there, I will be there; if not, I will not go."

21:21 Yisrael sent emissaries to Sichon king of the Amorites with the following message.

YISRAEL SENT EMISSARIES—Elsewhere, the sending [of these emissaries] is attributed to Moshe [rather than Yisrael,] as it says, *I sent emissaries from the desert of Kedeimos* (*Devarim* 2:26). Similarly, *Moshe sent emissaries to the king of Edom* (ibid. 20:14), and [referring to this incident Yiftach said, *Yisrael sent messengers to the king of Edom* (*Shofetim* 11:17). These verses complement each other; one verse holds back [information], and the other reveals. [By comparing these verses we infer] that Moshe is Yisrael, and Yisrael is Moshe. This teaches that the leader of the generation is equal to the entire generation, because the leader is everything.

בלק
BALAK

———◦◦◦———

22:4 Moav said to the elders of Midian, "Now the community [of B'nei Yisrael] will lick up our entire surrounding, just as a bull licks up all the vegetation in the field."

THE ELDERS OF MIDIAN—Weren't [Midian and Moav] eternal enemies? After all, Midian went to war against Moav, as it says, *who defeated Midian in the field of Moav* (*Bereishis* 36:35). Because of their mutual fear of Yisrael they made peace with each other.

What prompted Moav to seek advice from Midian? When they saw that Yisrael defeated [their enemies] in a supernatural way, they said, "[Moshe,] the leader of these [people] was raised in Midian. Let us ask them what kind of person he is." [The Midianites] told them, "His only power is with his mouth." [Thereupon the Moabites] said, "We too will confront them with a man whose strength is with his mouth [namely, Bilam who cursed effectively.]"

22:5 He sent emissaries to Bilam son of Beor, to his native land in Pesor on the [Euphrates] River. They were to summon him with the following message, "The nation that has left Egypt now covers the land's surface and is now staying near us."

TO HIS NATIVE LAND . . . If you ask, "Why did G-d bestow His Shechinah on a wicked heathen?" [The answer is:] So the nations should not have an excuse to say, "Would we have had prophets we would have repented." He therefore established prophets for them, but they breached the barrier of sexual morality. At first they refrained from promiscuity, but [Bilam] advised them to offer themselves freely for immorality.

22:8 "Spend the night here," he replied to them, "and I will give you an answer when G-d speaks to me." The Moabite dignitaries stayed with Bilam.

SPEND THE NIGHT HERE—He [Bilam] only had Divine inspiration at night; this applies to all non-Jewish prophets. So too, [G-d came to] Lavan in a dream at night, as it says, *G-d appeared to Lavan the Aramaean that night in a dream* (*Bereishis* 31:24), like a man furtively going to his concubine.

22:18 Bilam responded to Balak's servants and said, "Even if Balak would give me his whole palace full of gold and silver, I would not be able to do anything great or small that would violate the word of Hashem, my G-d."

I WOULD NOT BE ABLE TO DO ANYTHING . . . THAT WOULD VIOLATE—He grudgingly admitted that he was controlled by others. Here he prophesied that he could not undo the blessings the Shechinah bestowed on the patriarchs.

22:21 Bilam got up early in the morning and saddled his female donkey. He went with the Midianite dignitaries.

AND SADDLED HIS FEMALE DONKEY—From here [we learn] that hatred causes one to disregard refined conduct, for he saddled the donkey himself. The Holy One, blessed be He, said, "Wicked one! Their father Avraham has already preceded you, as it says, *Avraham got up early in the morning and saddled his donkey* (*Bereishis* 22:3), [to do the will of G-d.]"

22:23 The donkey saw G-d's angel standing in the road with a drawn sword in his hand. The donkey veered from the road into the field. Bilam beat the donkey to get it back on the road.

THE DONKEY SAW G-D'S ANGEL—But [Bilam] did not see it, for G-d gave animals the power to see more than man [can see]. Since [man] has intelligence, he would become insane if he saw demons [or angels].

A DRAWN SWORD IN HIS HAND—[The angel] said: This wicked man has forsaken the tool of his trade, for the weapon of the nations of the world is the sword, and he is coming against [Yisrael] with the [power of the] mouth, which is [Yisrael's] forte. I too, will adopt his [profession], attacking him with his own craft. This was indeed his end, as it says, *They slew Bilam son of Beor with the sword* (31:8).

23:4 G-d happened upon Bilam, and [Bilam] said to [G-d], "I have set up the seven altars, and I brought a bull and a ram as a burnt offering on each altar."

G-D HAPPENED UPON TO BILAM—The Hebrew word for "happened upon" is, *vayikor,* which denotes a casual meeting, suggesting something shameful, akin to the pollution of a seminal emission, [which has the same Hebrew root—*keri.*] The implication is that G-d appeared to Bilam reluctantly and with contempt, only appearing to him by day to show His love for Yisrael.

I HAVE SET UP THE SEVEN ALTARS—He did not say: "I have set up seven altars," but rather, *I have set up the seven altars.* He said [to G-d], "Their patriarchs built seven altars before You, and I have prepared seven altars to match them all."

Avraham built four [altars, as it says,] *There he built an altar to Hashem who appeared to him* (*Bereishis* 12:7); *Avraham moved from there to the mountain . . . and built an altar there* (ibid. 12:8);

Avraham pitched his tent and built an altar there (ibid. 13:18); and one altar [he built] on Mount Moriah (ibid. 22:9).

Yitzchak built one altar, as it says, *He built an altar there* (ibid. 26:25). Yaakov built two altars, one in Shechem (ibid. 33:20) and one in Beth El (ibid. 35:7).

23:8 What curse can I pronounce, if G-d will not grant a curse? What divine wrath can I conjure, if G-d will not be angry?

WHAT CURSE CAN I PRONOUNCE IF G-D WILL NOT GRANT A CURSE?—Even when they [the Jewish people] deserved to be cursed, they were not cursed. When their father [Yaakov] recalled their sin, [saying,] *For in their wrath they killed a man* (*Bereishis* 49:6), he cursed only their wrath, [but not themselves], as it says, *Cursed be their wrath* (ibid. 7).

When their father [Yaakov] came with deceit to his father [Yitzchak], he deserved to be cursed. But what does it say there? *He too, shall be blessed* (ibid.27:33).

Regarding the [tribes] that stood to be blessed, it says, *These shall stand to bless the people* (*Devarim* 21:12). However, regarding the [tribes] that stood by the curse, it does not say, "These shall stand to curse the people," rather, *These shall stand for the curse* (ibid. 21:13), for G-d does not want to mention the word "curse" in reference to B'nei Yisrael.

23:9 I see them[8] from the mountaintops and gaze on them from the heights. It is a nation dwelling alone, not counted among the other nations.

I SEE THEM FROM THE MOUNTAINTOPS—Looking at their origins and the beginning of their roots, I see them established and powerful, because of their patriarch and matriarchs.

---

8   The Jewish people.

IT IS A NATION DWELLING ALONE—This [nation's] forefathers gained for them the privilege to dwell alone.

NOT BEING COUNTED AMONG THE OTHER NATIONS—The Targum translates: They will not perish along with the other nations, as it says, *For I will bring annihilation upon all the nations among whom I have dispersed you, but upon you I will not bring annihilation* (*Yirmeyah* 30:11).

Another interpretation: When [Yisrael] rejoices no other nation will rejoice with them, as it says, *G-d will lead [Yisrael] alone* (*Devarim* 32:12). And when the nations prosper, [Yisrael] will share the bounty with each one of them, yet this will not be deducted [from the reward for their mitzvos and good deeds] that is in store for them. This is the meaning of, *not being counted among the other nations.*

23:10 Who can count the dust of Yaakov, and number the seed of Yisrael? Let me die the death of the upright, and let my end be like his.

WHO CAN COUNT THE DUST OF YAAKOV—As the Targum translates: Who can count the children of the house of Yaakov about whom it says, *They shall be as numerous as the dust of the earth. . .*

Another interpretation: [*Who can count*] *the dust of Yaakov*— means the mitzvos they do with dust cannot be counted. [For example]:

Do not plow with an ox and a donkey [harnessed together] (*Devarim* 22:10);

Do not sow your field with a mixture of seeds (*Vayikra* 19:19);

The ashes of the red cow (*Bamidbar* chapter 19);

The dust used for a woman suspected of infidelity (*Bamidbar* 5:17), and similar mitzvos.

23:21 [G-d] does not look at wrongdoing in Yaakov, and He sees no vice in Yisrael. Hashem their G-d is with them, and they have the King's friendship.

[G-D] DOES NOT LOOK AT WRONGDOING IN YAAKOV—The Targum translates this [to mean:] I have looked and seen no idol worshippers in Yaakov.

Its literal meaning can be expounded beautifully: The Holy One, blessed be He, does not look at wrongdoing [that may occur] in Yaakov. When they transgress His word He does not painstakingly scrutinize their wicked deeds to delve into their iniquity in violating His law.

HASHEM THEIR G-D IS WITH THEM—Even if they anger Him and rebel against Him, He does not budge from their midst.

AND THEY HAVE THE KING'S FRIENDSHIP Onkelos translates this phrase as, "the *Shechinah* of their King is among them."

23:23 There is no black magic in Yaakov, and no occult powers in Yisrael. In time it will be said to Yaakov and Yisrael, "How is G-d acting?"

THERE IS NO BLACK MAGIC IN YAAKOV—They are worthy of blessing, because there are no diviners and soothsayers among them.

IN TIME IT WILL BE SAID TO YAAKOV AND YISRAEL, "HOW IS G-D ACTING?"—There will be another time like this, when the love [G-d has for Yisrael] will be revealed to all, when they will sit before Him, learning Torah from His mouth. They will be closer [to the *Shechinah*] than the ministering angels. [The angels] will ask them, "How is G-d acting?" This is implied by the phrase, *Your eyes shall behold your teacher* (*Yeshayah* 30:20).

Another interpretation: This phrase is not in the future tense, rather it is in the present tense. [Thus the meaning is:] They have no need for a diviner or sorcerer. Whenever it is necessary to tell Yaakov and Yisrael how G-d is acting and what decrees He has enacted on high, they need not resort to divining or soothsaying, for the decrees of G-d are transmitted to them by their prophets, or they are informed by the Urim and Tumim.

23:24

This is a nation that rises like a lion cub, and lifts itself like a lion. It does not lie down until it eats its prey and drinks the blood of its kill.

THIS IS A NATION THAT RISES LIKE A LION CUB—When they awaken from their sleep in the morning, they energize themselves like a lion cub and a lion to grasp the mitzvos, putting on the tallis, reading the *Shema,* and putting on tefillin.

IT DOES NOT LIE DOWN—[A Jew] does not lie down at night until he consumes and destroys any harmful thing that comes to destroy him. How so? He recites the Bedtime Shema, entrusting his spirit to the Omnipresent. Should an army or a horde [of bandits] come to harm him, the Holy One, blessed be He, protects [him], fighting his battles, and obliterating [his attackers].

פינחס

PINCHAS

---•◦•---

26:1 It was after the plague. Hashem spoke to Moshe and to Elazar son of Aharon the kohein, saying:

IT WAS AFTER THE PLAGUE—[After the plague, G-d ordered a census to be taken.] This can be compared to a shepherd whose flock was overrun by wolves that killed some of [his sheep]. He counted them to know how many were left.

Another interpretation: When [B'nei Yisrael] left Egypt and were entrusted to Moshe they were handed to him by number. Now that he was close to death and returning his flock, he returned them by number.

26:5 Reuven was Yisrael's firstborn. The descendants of Reuven were: Chanoch of the HaChanoch'i family, Palu of the HaPalu'i family.

CHANOCH OF THE HA'CHANOCHI FAMILY—Because the nations vilified [B'nei Yisrael], saying, "How can they trace their ancestry by tribes? Do they think the Egyptians did not attack their mothers? If they mastered their bodies, they surely subdued their wives!"

Therefore, the Holy One, blessed be He, attached His name to [their names,] with the letter *hei* on one side and the letter *yud* on the other side, [turning Chanoch into HaChanochi, Palu into

Hapalui], declaring, "I testify for them that they are the sons of their [Jewish] fathers [and not of Egyptians]."

This is expressed explicitly by David, *The tribes of Υ-ah, a testimony for Yisrael* (*Tehillim* 122:4)—This name [*yud-hei*] testifies to [the purity of] their tribes. For this reason, the Torah adds [a *hei* and a *yud*] to each name: HaChanochi, Hapalui. It was not necessary to say HaYumnai, by the name Yimnah, because G-d's name is already part of [that name], with a *yud* at the beginning and a *hei* at the end.

26:64 Among those [counted here] there was no man [previously] counted by Moshe and Aharon the kohein, who had taken a census of B'nei Yisrael in the Sinai Desert.

AMONG THOSE [COUNTED HERE] THERE WAS NO MAN [PREVIOUSLY] COUNTED—But the women were not included in the decree regarding the spies, for they cherished Eretz Yisrael. When the men said, "*Let us appoint a [new] leader and return to Egypt*" (14:4), the women said, "*Give us a portion of the Land*" (27:4). Therefore the chapter of Tzelofchad's daughters [who desired a share of the land] follows.

27:1 A petition[9] was presented by the daughters of Tzelofchad, son of Chefer, son of Gilad, son of Menasheh, of the family of Yosef's son Menasheh. The names of his daughters were Machlah, Noah, Choglah, Milkah and Tirtzah.

OF THE FAMILY OF YOSEF'S SON MENASHEH—Why does the Torah repeat that they were descendants of Yosef's son Menasheh? After all, it already says [that Tzelofchad's five daughters were descen-

---

9   Their father had died without sons to inherit his portion in the land, they petitioned that they should inherit his portion.

dants of] *the son of Menasheh?* To tell you [that Tzelofchad's daughters inherited a love of Eretz Yisrael from their ancestor] Yosef who cherished Eretz Yisrael, for he said, *[When you leave Egypt] you must bring my remains out of here with you* (Shemos 13:19). His granddaughters also cherished Eretz Yisrael, as it says, *Give us a portion of the land* (27:4).

[Furthermore,] it teaches that all [the individuals mentioned in this verse] were righteous. If the Torah details anyone whose deeds and whose father's deeds are unknown, tracing his ancestry for praise, [that means] he is a righteous man, the son of a righteous man. But if [the Torah] traces his ancestry for shame, as for example, *Yishmael the son of Nesanyah the son of Elishama came* (2 *Melachim* 25:25), that means all those mentioned with him were wicked people.

27:13 You will see [the Land] and then you will be gathered up to your people, just as your brother Aharon was gathered.

JUST AS YOUR BROTHER AHARON WAS GATHERED—From here it is evident that Moshe yearned to die as Aharon did.

Another explanation [why Moshe was compared to Aharon. G-d said:] You are no better than he, *because you did not sanctify Me* [at the Waters of Dispute]. Had you sanctified Me, your time to leave the world would not have arrived.

Whenever their death is mentioned, their sin is mentioned. Because a decree had been pronounced against the generation of the desert that they die in the desert because of their sin [of believing the bad report of the spies] and not believing [that G-d would give them Eretz Yisrael]. Moshe, therefore, requested that his sin [at *Mei Merivah*] be mentioned, so it should not be said he was one of those who rebelled [in the wake of the report of the spies]. This is comparable to the case of two women who were given lashes by the *beis din*. One woman was guilty of adultery, and the other ate unripe figs of the sabbatical year. [The later offense is not nearly as grave as the former.]

The woman [who had eaten the unripe figs] requested that a string of fruit of the sabbatical year be tied around her neck, so people should know she was being flogged for eating such fruit, rather than for adultery. Here too, wherever the death [of Moshe and Aharon] is mentioned, their sin is spelled out clearly, to let you know their only sin was the sin [of *Mei Merivah*].

27:15,16 Moshe spoke to Hashem, saying: "Let the Omnipresent G-d of all souls appoint a man over the community."

MOSHE SPOKE TO HASHEM, SAYING—This verse lets us know the virtues of the righteous; when they are about to depart the world they set aside their own needs, involving themselves with the needs of the community.

LET THE OMNIPRESENT G-D OF ALL SOULS APPOINT A MAN OVER THE COMMUNITY—When Moshe heard G-d telling him to give Tzelofchad's inheritance to his daughters, he said, "The time has come to ask for my own needs; that my sons should inherit my high post."

The Holy One, blessed be He, told him, "That is not whom I have in mind. Yehoshua deserves to be rewarded for his service, for *he never left the tent* (*Shemos* 33:11)." This is what Shelomoh meant when he said, *He who guards the fig tree will enjoy its fruit* (*Mishlei* 27:18).

THE OMNIPRESENT G-D OF ALL SOULS—[Moshe] said to G-d, "You know the mindset of each person, and You know that no two persons think alike. Appoint for them a leader who will accept each person according to his individual personality."

27:17 Let him come and go before them, and let him bring them forth and lead them. Don't let Hashem's community be like sheep that have no shepherd.

LET HIM GO BEFORE THEM—[The leader] should not be like the kings of the [gentile] nations who sit at home, sending their armies to war. Rather [he should do] as I did, for I fought against Sichon and Og, as it says, [Hashem said to Moshe,] *Do not be afraid of [Og but kill him as you killed Sichon]* (21:34), and as Yehoshua did, as it says, *Yehoshua went [forth to the angel] and said to him, "Are you with us [or with our enemies]?"* (*Yehoshua* 5:13).

Similarly, it says about David, *For he went forth and came in before them* (1 *Shemuel* 18:16)—he went out to battle at the head [of his army] and came in before them.

LET HIM BRING THEM FORTH—through his merits; and lead them—through his merits.

Another interpretation: *Let him bring them forth*—[Allow him to lead them into Eretz Yisrael,] not as You did to me, not allowing me to bring them into the Land.

27:18 Hashem said to Moshe, "Take Yehoshua son of Nun, a man of spirit, and lay your hands on him."

TAKE YEHOSHUA SON OF NUN—Persuade him [to accept the leadership] by saying, "Fortunate are you that you have merited to lead the children of the Omnipresent!"

27:19 Have him stand before Elazar the kohein and before the entire community, and command him in front of them.

AND COMMAND HIM IN FRONT OF THEM—concerning Yisrael. [Tell Yehoshua,] "Be aware that they are troublesome and stubborn. [You can only become their leader] if you take this upon yourself."

27:22 Moshe did as Hashem had ordered him. He took Yehoshua and had him stand before Elazar the kohein and before the entire community.

HE TOOK YEHOSHUA—He took him [by persuading him] with words, letting him know the reward that awaits the leaders of B'nei Yisrael in the World to Come.

27:23 He then laid his hands on him and commissioned him. [It was all done] as Hashem had commanded Moshe.

HE THEN LAID HIS HANDS ON HIM—with generosity, over and above what he had been told. For the Holy One, blessed be He, told him, *Lay your hand on him* (27:10), but he did it with both hands, making [Yehoshua] a full and overflowing vessel, filling him with an abundance of wisdom.

28:2 Give B'nei Yisrael instructions and tell them, "Be careful to offer My fire-offering food to Me in its proper time as My appeasing fragrance."

GIVE B'NEI YISRAEL INSTRUCTIONS—What [is the connection between the daily sacrifice and] what it says above, [that Moshe asked G-d to appoint a leader for the people,] saying, *Let G-d appoint a man over the community* (27:16)?

The Holy One, blessed be he, said to [Moshe], "Instead of telling Me what to do for My children, tell My children what they should do for Me, [namely, to obey My commandments.]"

This may be compared to a princess who was about to depart this world and instructed her husband about the children. [He replied, "Instead of instructing me about them, instruct them how to treat me."]

29:18 Along with the grain offering and the libations appropriate for the number of bulls, rams, and sheep.

ALONG WITH THE GRAIN OFFERING AND THE LIBATIONS APPROPRIATE FOR THE NUMBER OF BULLS, RAMS, AND SHEEP. . . The seventy bulls of Sukkos [of which each day a smaller number was offered] correspond to the seventy nations which will gradually diminish in number—a harbinger of their eventual disappearance. In the days of the Beis Hamikdash the sacrifices protected [the seventy nations] from misfortune.

AND SHEEP—[the sheep] correspond to Yisrael who are called *a scattered sheep* (*Yirmeyah* 50:17). [Fourteen sheep were offered each day of Sukkos,] for a total of ninety-eight [sheep], to cancel the ninety-eight curses in *Devarim* (28:5-68).

29:35 The eighth day shall be a time of restraint for you, and you shall do no mundane work.

A TIME OF RESTRAINT—when you shall be restrained from working.

Another interpretation: Restrain yourself from leaving. This teaches that one [may not leave immediately after Yom Tov, rather he] is required to stay [in Yerushalayim] overnight.

An Aggadic Midrash explains: Throughout the Yom Tov they brought [seventy] offerings, corresponding to the seventy nations [of the world, to make atonement for them]. When they were about to leave, G-d said to them, "Please make a simple meal for me, so I may enjoy your company [alone]."

29:36 As a burnt fire offering for an appeasing fragrance to Hashem, you shall present one bull, one ram, and seven yearling sheep without blemish.

ONE BULL, ONE RAM—[As opposed to the other days of Sukkos where many bulls rams and sheep were brought corresponding to the seventy nations of the world, the offerings of this day] correspond to Yisrael. [Thus G-d says,] "Stay with Me a little longer." This shows His love [for Yisrael], like children taking leave of their father who says to them, "It is difficult for me to part with you. Please stay one more day."

מטות

MATTOS

———⚫———

VOWS

30:6 However, if he obstructs her on the day he hears it[10], then any such vow or self-imposed obligation of hers shall not be fulfilled. Since her father has obstructed her, Hashem will forgive her.

HASHEM WILL FORGIVE HER—To what case is the verse referring? A woman made a nazirite vow, which her husband heard and revoked without her knowledge. She then violated her vow by drinking wine and becoming unclean through contact with corpses. This woman requires forgiveness even though [her vow] was revoked, [and she did not sin].

Now if vows that have been revoked require forgiveness, surely those that have not been revoked [require forgiveness when broken].

30:16 However, if he annuls [her vows] after [the allotted time, after] he heard them, [and she violated the vow thinking his annulment was valid] he shall bear her guilt.

———

[10] If a woman makes a vow and her father or husband hears of it, he may revoke the vow on that day.

AFTER HE HEARD THEM, HE SHALL BEAR HER GUILT—He takes her place. We learn from here that if someone causes his fellow to stumble, he takes their place regarding all punishment.

31:2,3 Take revenge for B'nei Yisrael against the Midianites, then you [Moshe, shall die] and be gathered to your people. Moshe spoke to the people, saying, "Draft men for armed service against Midian, so Hashem's revenge shall be taken against the Midianites."

MOSHE SPOKE TO THE PEOPLE—Although he heard that his death was dependant on the matter [of making war against Midian], he did it joyfully, without delay.

HASHEM'S REVENGE—For whoever fights against Yisrael fights against the Holy One, blessed be He.

31:5 From the thousands of Yisrael, one thousand were recruited from each tribe. Twelve thousand armed for war.

ONE THOUSAND WERE RECRUITED—[Since it does not say, "one thousand volunteered," we can deduce that the men were forced to go to war. By implication] we see the praise of the shepherds of Yisrael, and how beloved they were to Yisrael. For before [the people] heard that Moshe would die, [Moshe] said, *Before long they will stone me* (*Shemos* 17:4), [proving that the people were very angry with him]. But when they heard that Moshe's death was tied to the revenge against Midian, they refused to go, until they were drafted against their will.

31:8 Along with the other victims, they killed the five kings of Midian: Evi, Rekem, Tzur, Chur, and Reva. They also killed Bilam son of Beor by the sword.

THEY ALSO KILLED BILAM BY THE SWORD—He came against Yisrael exchanging his specialty [the sword] for Yisrael's forte, [the voice of prayer and blessing,] for [Yisrael] is triumphant only with their mouths through prayer and supplication. [Bilam] came and usurped their forte by cursing them with his mouth, so they attacked him by exchanging their specialty with the specialty of the nations who come with the sword, as it says [about Eisav], *You shall live by your sword* (*Bereishis* 27:40).

31:14 Moshe became angry at the generals and the captains who were the officers returning from the military campaign.

MOSHE BECAME ANGRY AT THE GENERALS AND THE CAPTAINS— Those appointed over the army. This comes to teach that the leaders are to blame for the sins of the people, for they have the power to deter them.

31:21 Elazar the kohein said to the soldiers returning from the campaign, "This is the rule that Hashem commanded Moshe."

ELAZAR THE KOHEIN—Since Moshe became angry, he forgot the laws of removing the non-kosher tastes absorbed in the utensils.

A similar incident happened on the eighth day of the ordination [of the kohanim], as it says, *He [Moshe] became angry at Elazar and Isamar* (*Vayikra* 10:16); since he became angry, he erred.

Similarly, in the episode [when Moshe angrily exclaimed,] *"Listen now, you rebels!"* (20:10,11), he [made the error of] striking the rock [instead of speaking to it]. His anger caused him to make the error.

מסעי

MASAI

———◆◆◆———

33:1 These are the journeys of B'nei Yisrael who had left Egypt in organized groups under the leadership of Moshe and Aharon.

THESE ARE THE JOURNEYS—Why were these journeys recorded? To let us know G-d's kindness. Although He decreed that [B'nei Yisrael] wander in the wilderness, do not think they were constantly on the move from place to place, without letup for the entire forty years. [Proof of this is that] there are listed only forty-two journeys. Subtract fourteen, for these took place in the first year, before the decree [of the spies], when they traveled from Raamses until they arrived in Rismah. From there the spies were sent [in the first year], as it says, *The people then left Chatzeiros and camped in the Desert of Paran* (12:16), [followed by,] *Send out men for yourself to explore . . .* (13:2), and here it says, *They left Chatzeiros and camped in Rismah* (33:13), which teaches us that Rismah is in the Desert of Paran.

Subtract another eight journeys which took place after Aharon's death, [when they traveled] from Mount Hor to the Plains of Moav in the fortieth year, and you will find that throughout the [remaining] thirty-eight years they made only twenty journeys.

34:2 Give B'nei Yisrael instructions and say to them: You are coming to the land of Canaan; this is the land

that shall fall as your hereditary territory, the land of Canaan
in its borders.

THIS IS THE LAND . . . THAT SHALL FALL TO YOUR AS YOUR HERED-
ITARY TERRITORY—. . . The Midrash Aggadah says [the term "shall
fall"] is used here, because the Holy One, blessed be He, caused
the heavenly guardians of the seven [Canaanite] nations to fall. He
shackled them before Moshe, saying, "See, they are powerless."

35:25 The court shall protect the [accidental] murderer
from the blood avenger, and return him to the
refuge city to which he fled. [The killer] must live there until
the death of the Kohein Gadol, who was anointed with the sacred oil.

UNTIL THE DEATH OF THE KOHEIN GADOL—For [the Kohein
Gadol] causes the *Shechinah* to rest on Yisrael, thus prolonging
their lives, whereas the murderer causes the *Shechinah* to withdraw
from Yisrael, thus shortening their lives. [Therefore, the murderer]
does not deserve to stand before the Kohein Gadol.

   Another explanation: The Kohein Gadol should have prayed
that such a misfortune not happen in Yisrael during his lifetime.

35:34 You must not defile the land upon which you live
and in which I dwell, since I, Hashem, dwell
among B'nei Yisrael.

THE LAND UPON WHICH YOU LIVE AND IN WHICH I DWELL—You
should not cause Me to dwell in impurity.

SINCE I, HASHEM, DWELL AMONG B'NEI YISRAEL—Even when
[B'nei Yisrael] are unclean the *Shechinah* dwells among them.

דברים
DEVARIM

———◆———

1:6 Hashem our G-d spoke to us at Chorev, saying: "You have remained very long at this mountain [of Sinai]."

YOU HAVE REMAINED VERY LONG AT THIS MOUNTAIN—[This is the translation] according to its simple meaning. The Aggadic explanation [translates the words as follows: *You have gained much by remaining at this mountain*—G-d] granted you much eminence and reward while at this mountain. You made the Mishkan, the Menorah, and [other] furnishings. You received the Torah, and you appointed a Sanhedrin for yourselves, with judges over thousands and over hundreds.

1:8 See! I have placed the land before you. Come and occupy the land that Hashem swore He would give to your forefathers, Avraham, Yitzchak, and Yaakov, and to their descendants after them.

COME AND OCCUPY—No one will resist you, neither will you have to go to war [in order to conquer the land]. Had [B'nei Yisrael relied on G-d's promise and] not sent the spies, they would not have needed weapons.

TO YOUR FOREFATHERS—[Having said *your forefathers*] why does [the Torah continue to] specify, Avraham, Yitzchak, and Yaakov?

79

[Their names are mentioned] to show that Avraham alone is worthy [of the promise], Yitzchak alone is worthy, and Yaakov alone is worthy.

1:9 I said to you at that time, "I cannot bear you alone."

I CANNOT BEAR YOU ALONE—Is it conceivable that Moshe was unable to judge Yisrael? The man who brought them out of Egypt, split the sea for them, brought down the manna, and brought the quail, could not judge them?

Rather, he said to them as follows: *Hashem, your G-d has increased you*—making you great, and raising you over your judges. He took punishment away from you, imposing it on the judges.

Shelomoh made a similar statement, saying, *For who is able to judge this formidable people of Yours* (1 *Melachim* 5:11). Is it possible that the one of whom it is said, *And [Shelomoh] became wiser than any man* (ibid. 3:9) would say, *For who is able to judge . . .?*

Rather, Shelomoh said: The judges of this nation are not like the judges of other nations. If [a judge of the other nations] kills, beats, strangles, perverts judgment, or robs, it does not matter, [and he is not responsible for his unjust decision. However,] if I wrongly sentence a person to pay money, I am liable for my very life, as it says, *He takes the life of those who steal from them* (*Mishlei* 22:23).

1:10 Hashem your G-d has increased your numbers until you are today as the many stars in the sky.

YOU ARE TODAY AS THE MANY STARS IN THE SKY—Were they like the stars of the sky on that day? After all, they were only six hundred thousand. What is meant by *you are today as the many stars of the sky*? You are likened to the day, lasting forever like the sun, the moon and the stars.

1:11 May Hashem, the G-d of your fathers, increase your numbers a thousand fold and bless you as He promised.

MAY HASHEM, THE G-D OF YOUR FATHERS, INCREASE YOUR NUM-
BERS A THOUSAND FOLD—Why [does Moshe repeat,] *and bless you
as He has promised*? [When Moshe gave this blessing, the people]
said to him: "Moshe, you are putting a ceiling [of "a thousand
fold"] on our blessings, [while] the Holy One, blessed be He, has
already promised Avraham, *If a man will be able to count [all] the
grains of dust in the world, then your offspring, too, can be counted*
(*Bereishis* 13:16) [which is a blessing without limitation]."

Moshe replied, "The blessing [of a thousand fold] is my [bless-
ing]; but, *He will bless you as He promised,* [with an unlimited blessing.]

1:13 Designate for yourselves men who are wise, understanding, and known to your tribes, and I will appoint
them as your leaders.

AND I WILL APPOINT THEM AS YOUR LEADERS—The words *and I
will appoint—va'asimeim*—is written without a *yud* [between the
sin and *men*; thus it can be read *v'asham*, which means guilt]. This
teaches that the guilt of [the sinners of] Yisrael falls on the heads of
their leaders, who should have prevented them [from committing
sins,] directing them on the right path.

1:15 I took wise and well-known men from among your
tribal leaders, and appointed them as your leaders—
captains of thousands, captains of hundreds, captains of fifties,
and captains of tens, and police for your tribes.

I TOOK—FROM AMONG YOUR TRIBAL LEADERS—I won them over
with [convincing] words, saying, "How fortunate are you! Over
whom are you being appointed? Over the sons of Avraham,
Yitzchak, and Yaakov; a people who are called *brothers and friends*
[of Hashem,] *the portion and inheritance* [of Hashem], and similar
expressions of love."

1:16 I gave your judges instructions at that time, saying, "Listen [to every dispute] among your brothers, and judge justly between man and his brother, and his litigant."

I GAVE YOUR JUDGES INSTRUCTIONS—I said to them, "Be patient when passing judgment. If a case comes before you once, twice, and even thrice, do not say, "This kind of case has already come before me many times." Rather deliberate over it.

AT THAT TIME—After appointing them I told them, "Today things are not for you as they were in the past. In the past you were your own masters. Now you are subject [to the will of] the community."

1:17 Do not give anyone special consideration when rendering judgment. Listen to small and great alike. Do not be afraid of any man since judgment is to G-d. If any case is too difficult for you, bring it to me, and I will hear it.

LISTEN TO SMALL AND GREAT ALIKE—A case involving the value of a small *perutah* coin shall be as important to you as a case involving a hundred gold *maneh* coins. Thus, if [the case involving the *perutah*] came before you first, do not put it off for the last.

Another explanation: Understand *Listen to small and great alike* as the Targum translates it—[*small* and *great* refers to the poor and rich man.] Do not say to yourself, "This one is poor, and his antagonist is rich. Since it is a mitzvah [for the rich] to support [the poor], I will rule in favor of the poor man, so he will be supported in a respectable manner."

Another explanation: Do not say to yourself, "How can I humiliate this rich man for the sake of one *dinar*. Let me rule in his favor now, and when he goes out I will tell him, "Give [the *dinar*] to the poor man, because you really owe it to him."

SINCE JUDGMENT IS TO G-D—Whatever you, [the judge,] take from someone unjustly, I am forced to restore to him. Thus, you have cast the judgment on Me.

BRING IT TO ME, AND I WILL HEAR IT—[Moshe should have said, "Bring it to G-d, and He will hear it."] Because of this [seemingly haughty statement] Moshe forgot the law concerning the [inheritance of the] daughters of Tzelofchad (*Bamidbar* 27:1-5).

Similarly, Shemuel said to Shaul, *"I am the seer"* (1 *Shemuel* 9:19), whereupon the Holy One, blessed be He, said to him, "I swear by your life that I will show to you, that you do not [always] see." When did He show him? When he came to anoint David, as it says, *He, [Shemuel], saw Eliav,* [Yishai's son] *and said, "Certainly His anointed one is standing before Hashem"* (1 *Shemuel* 16:6.7). The Holy One, blessed be He, said to him, "Did you not say, 'I am the seer?' [You are wrong.] *Do not look at his appearance and the height of his stature, for I have rejected him* (ibid. 16:6,7)."

SENDING THE SPIES

1:23 The matter met with my approval, and I appointed twelve men, one for each tribe.

THE MATTER MET WITH MY APPROVAL—It met with my approval, but not with G-d's approval. If Moshe approved [of their request to send spies], why did he include this in his reproof of Yisrael?

This can be compared to one who asks his neighbor, "Will you sell me this donkey?"

He replies, "Yes."

"Will you let me test it?"

"Yes,"

"May I test it on mountains and hills?"

Again he replies, "Yes."

Because he does not deny [any requests], the buyer thinks, "He must be certain I will not find anything wrong with the donkey." He immediately says, "Take your money. I do not need to test it."

[Said Moshe,] "I too, agreed to your request [to send spies], hoping you might reconsider when you saw I did not stand in your way. But you did not change your mind."

1:27 You spread false rumors in your tents, and said, "Hashem brought us out of Egypt because He hated us! He wanted to turn us over to the Amorites to destroy us!"

BECAUSE HE HATED US—In fact, He really loved you, but you hated Him. A popular saying has it, "What is in your heart about your friend is what [you think] is in his heart about you."

2:16,17 It was when all the men of war among the people finished dying, that Hashem spoke to me, saying.

ALL THE MEN OF WAR . . . FINISHED DYING, THAT HASHEM SPOKE TO ME—But from the time the spies were sent until now, the Torah does not say, "Hashem spoke to Moshe" [in a loving manner.] It only says, "Hashem said," [speaking in a detached manner]. This teaches that during the entire thirty-eight years B'nei Yisrael were scorned [by G-d], G-d did not speak to [Moshe] intimately, in loving terms, face to face, and with serenity. This teaches that the *Shechinah* rests upon the prophets only for the sake of Yisrael. [And when Yisrael is spurned, G-d does not communicate lovingly with His prophets.]

2:26 I sent emissaries from the Kedeimos Desert to Sichon, king of Cheshbon, with a peaceful message, saying.

I SENT EMISSARIES FROM THE KEDEIMOS DESERT—Although the Omnipresent did not command me to propose peace to Sichon, I learned to do so from [Hashem's actions] in the Desert of Sinai, as related in the Torah, which preceded[11] the [creation of the] world.

When the Holy One, blessed be He, came to give the Torah to Yisrael, He first offered it to Eisav and Yishmael. Although it was clear to Him that they would not accept it, nonetheless, He initi-

---

[11] The root of the word *Kedeimos* is *Kedem*, which means preceded.

ated a peace proposal. I too, advanced toward Sichon with a peace initiative.

Another explanation: *from the Kedeimos Desert* implies that [Moshe said to G-d:] I learned from You Who preceded the world. You could have sent forth one lightning bolt to incinerate the Egyptians, but instead, You sent me from the desert to Pharaoh with the message, "Let my people go!" acting with patience.

3:2 Hashem said to me, "Do not be afraid of him [Og] since I have placed him in your hands along with all his people and his land. You will do the same to him as you did to the Amorite king Sichon, who lived in Cheshbon."

DO NOT BE AFRAID OF [OG]—But when he prepared to [attack] Sichon it was not necessary to say, "Do not be afraid of him." Moshe was afraid that the merit of the service [Og] had rendered to Avraham might stand him in good stead, as it says, *The fugitive came* [to inform Avraham that his nephew Lot had been captured] (*Bereishis* 14:13). That fugitive was Og.

ואתחנן
VA'ESCHANAN

MOSHE'S PLEA TO ENTER ERETZ YISRAEL

3:23 I pleaded with Hashem at that time, saying.

I PLEADED—Pleading always denotes [a request for] a free gift. Although the tzaddikim could make requests on the basis of their good deeds, they ask only for a free gift from the Omnipresent.

3:24 O Hashem, G-d! You have begun to show your servant Your greatness and Your strong hand. What Force is there in heaven or on earth that can perform deeds and mighty acts as You can.

YOU HAVE BEGUN TO SHOW YOUR SERVANT—You hinted that I should start praying, although the decree [of my death] was already sealed.

[Moshe] said [to G-d:] I learned [this] from You, for [after the sin of the Golden Calf] You told me, *"And now, leave me alone"* (*Shemos* 32:10). Was I holding on to You? [You said this] to hint that it depended on my prayers [to save Yisrael from destruction,] or I could leave You alone [and let You destroy Yisrael]. Now too, I thought to do the same [and begin to pray].

YOUR STRONG HAND—This is Your right hand which is extended to everyone [who does *teshuvah*].

STRONG HAND—[it is strong] because You suppress with mercy the powerful Attribute of strict Justice.

WHAT FORCE IS THERE . . . THAT CAN PERFORM DEEDS—You cannot be compared to a king of flesh and blood who has advisers and ministers that restrain him when he wants to act with kindness and override his attribute [of strict justice]. You, have no one to stop You if You forgive me and cancel Your decree.

4:9 Only take heed and watch yourself very carefully, so that you do not forget the things[12] that your eyes saw. Do not let this memory leave your hearts, all the days of your lives. Teach [them] to your children and children's children.

ONLY TAKE HEED AND WATCH YOURSELF VERY CAREFULLY, SO THAT YOU DO NOT FORGET THE THINGS THAT YOUR EYES SAW—Only then, when you do not forget the *mitzvos* and you do them correctly, will you be considered wise and understanding. But if you forget and do not do them properly, you will be considered fools.

5:24 You [Moshe] should approach Hashem our G-d[13] and listen to all He says. You can transmit to us whatever Hashem our G-d tells you, and when we hear it we will do it.

YOU CAN TRANSMIT TO US—[The verse uses *at* the feminine form of the word *you*. Moshe said,] "You weakened my strength [so that I became] like a woman. You gave me anguish, weakening my hand, for I saw that you were not eager to bring yourselves close

---

12 The mitzvos of the Torah.
13 During the giving of the Ten Commandments, the Jews requested from Moshe that Hashem not speak directly to them.

to Him out of love. Would it not have been better for you to learn directly from the mouth of the Almighty rather than from me?

THE SHEMA

6:4 Listen Yisrael, Hashem is our G-d. Hashem is One.

HASHEM IS OUR G-D. HASHEM IS ONE—Hashem who is our G-d now, but not the G-d of the other nations, will be the, "One and only G-d," in time to come. As it says, *For then I will change the nations [to speak] a clear language, so that they may all call out in the Name of Hashem* (*Tzefaniah* 3:9), and, *On that day Hashem will be One and His Name One* (*Zechariah* 14:9),

6:5 Love Hashem your G-d with all your heart, with all your soul, and with all your wealth.

LOVE HASHEM—Perform his commandments out of love. One who serves out of love cannot be compared to one who serves out of fear. If one serves his master out of fear, and [the master] makes him work too hard, he will quit going off by himself.

WITH ALL YOUR HEART—[You are to love G-d with] both your [good and evil] impulses.

Another explanation: *With all your heart* [means,] you should not challenge G-d in your heart, [if misfortune strikes].

WITH ALL YOUR SOUL—even if He takes your soul, [i.e., even if fulfilling His commandments costs you your life].

WITH ALL YOUR WEALTH—means, with all your money. There are people whose money is more precious to them than their own body. Therefore it says *with all your money.*

Another explanation: [The Hebrew word for *your wealth* is *me'odecha* which is related to the word *measure*. Thus the passage means:] Love G-d with whatever measure He metes out to you, whether it is the measure of goodness or the measure of punishment. In the same vein David said, *I will raise up a cup of salvation, [although] I found distress and anguish* (*Tehillim* 116:13).

6:6 These words that I am commanding you today must remain on your heart.

THESE WORDS . . . MUST REMAIN ON YOUR HEART—What is the love [of Hashem we are commanded in the previous verse]? It is that *these words* [the commandments] remain on our hearts, and thereby we will become aware of the Holy One, blessed be He, attaching ourselves to His ways.

THAT I AM COMMANDING YOU TODAY—[The word *today* implies that] you should not look at the Torah as an outdated royal document that no one cares about, but as a new one which everyone is eager to read.

6:7 Teach them (the words of Torah) to your children and speak of them when you are at home, when traveling on the road, when you lie down and when you get up.

TEACH THEM TO YOUR CHILDREN—[The Hebrew word for *teach* used here is *veshinnantam*, whose root is *shein*–tooth,] denoting sharpness. [The words of the Torah] should be sharp in your mouth; when a person asks you a question [about Torah,] you should not need to hesitate about it, but rather answer him immediately.

TO YOUR CHILDREN—These are the students. We find all over that students are called children, as it says, *You are children of Hashem your G-d* (*Devarim* 14:1) [meaning, you are students of Hashem], and, *The sons of the prophets who were in Bethel* (2 *Melachim* 2:3) [re-

ferring to students]. And so we find that Chezkiahu who taught
Torah to all Yisrael called them children, as it says, *My children do
not be negligent now* (2 *Divrei Hayamim* 29:11). And just as students are called children, so is the teacher called father, as it says,
[Elisha cried out at Eliyahu's death,] *My father, my father, chariot
of Yisrael!* (2 *Melachim* 2:12).

SPEAK OF THEM—[The implication is] that your conversation
should focus on [Torah and mitzvos]. Make them your major con-
cern rather than a side issue.

7:7 It is not because of you greatness [in numbers] over all
the other nations that Hashem desired you and chose
you; you are among the smallest of all the nations.

IT WAS NOT BECAUSE OF YOUR GREATNESS [IN NUMBERS]—
[Understand this] according to its plain meaning. Its Midrashic interpretation is: Because you do not gloat when I bestow goodness
on you, I desire you.

YOU ARE AMONG THE SMALLEST OF ALL THE NATIONS—You hum-
ble yourselves, like Avraham who said, *I am mere dust and ashes*
(*Bereishis* 18:27), and like Moshe and Aharon who said, *And what
are we?* (*Shemos* 16:7). This is unlike Nevuchadnetzar who said, *I
will liken myself to the Most High* (*Yeshayah* 14:14), and Sancheirev
who said, *Who among all the gods of these lands were able to save their
land from my hand, that Hashem should be able to save Yerushalayim
from my hand?* (ibid. 36:20), and Chiram who said, *I am a god; I
sat on the throne of G-d* (*Yechezkel* 28:2).

7:9 You must realize that Hashem your G-d is the Supreme
Being. He is the faithful G-d, who keeps in mind [His]
covenant and love for a thousand generations when it comes to
those who love Him and keep His commandments.

FOR A THOUSAND GENERATIONS—Elsewhere (above 5:10) it says, *for thousands* [of generations, in the plural. How can this seeming contradiction be reconciled?]

[This phrase] is adjacent to *those who keep His commandments*, [indicating that the merit of one who serves G-d out of fear endures only] *for a thousand generations*. But above, it refers to *those who love Me*. The reward for those who act out of love is *for thousands of generations*—a greater reward.

7:11 Safeguard the commandments, the rules and laws that I am commanding you today to do them.

TODAY TO DO THEM—[According to the cantillation marks, the word *today* does not modify *commanding you*, rather it modifies *to do them*.] Therefore, the meaning of the verse is: Today, [in this world,] you must do the mitzvos, and tomorrow, in the World to Come, you will receive reward.

עקב
EIKEV

————◆◇◆————

8:1 All the commandments that I am prescribing for you today you must safeguard and fulfill. You will then survive, flourish, and come to occupy the land that Hashem swore to your fathers.

ALL THE COMMANDMENTS—[Understand this] according to its simple meaning. However, the Midrash [translating the verse as *the entire commandment,*] suggests the following interpretation: If you have started a mitzvah be sure to finish it, since a *mitzvah* is only ascribed to the one who completes it. As it says, *And the remains of Yosef which B'nei Yisrael brought up from Egypt they buried in Shechem* (*Yehoshua* 24:32). Wasn't it Moshe alone who brought [Yosef's remains] up from Egypt? Because he was not able to carry out [Yosef's burial], and B'nei Yisrael completed it, it is ascribed to them.

8:4 The clothing you wore did not become tattered, and your feet did not swell these forty years.

THE CLOTHING YOU WORE DID NOT BECOME TATTERED—The Clouds of Glory smoothed and pressed their clothes, making them look like freshly ironed garments. And as their children grew, so did their clothing, like the shell of a snail which grows along with it.

MOSHE BEGS FORGIVENESS FOR THE SIN OF THE
GOLDEN CALF

9:18 I threw myself down before Hashem [on Mt. Sinai,] like the first time for forty days and forty nights. I did not eat any food nor drink water, because of your sins that you sinned to do what is evil in the eyes of Hashem to anger Him.

I THREW MYSELF DOWN BEFORE HASHEM—As [Moshe] said, *Now I will go back up to Hashem and try to get atonement for your crime* (*Shemos* 32:30). During that ascent I stayed [on the mountain] forty days. [The forty days] ended on the twenty-ninth of Av, for Moshe went up on the eighteenth of Tammuz. On that day, the Holy One, blessed be He, reconciled with Yisrael, saying to Moshe, *Carve out two tablets for yourself* (ibid. 34:1).

[Moshe] then spent another forty days [on the mountain] which ended on Yom Kippur, [the tenth of Tishri]. On that day, the Holy One, blessed be He, joyfully reconciled with Yisrael; saying to Moshe, *I have granted forgiveness as you have requested* (*Bamidbar* 14:20). That is why [Yom Kippur] was instituted [as the day] for forgiveness and pardon.

From where do we know that [G-d] reconciled with perfect goodwill? Regarding the forty days [Moshe was on the mountain preparing to bring down] the second set of Tablets he said, *I thus remained on the mountain forty days and forty nights, just like the first time* (*Devarim* 10:10). [He implied that] just as the [first] forty days were with goodwill [because Yisrael had not yet sinned,] so too, the last ones were with goodwill [for Yisrael was forgiven]. From this we may infer that the middle [forty days] were with [G-d's] anger.

10:7 From these areas they traveled to Gudgodah, and from Gudgodah to Yotvat, an area of flowing streams.

FROM GUDGODAH TO YOTVAT . . . At Moseirah you mourned deeply for the death of Aharon which was the cause of [the war with the Levites], and it seemed to you as if [Aharon] had died [in Moseirah].

[In the Torah] this reproof is juxtaposed with the breaking of the Tablets, to indicate that the death of the righteous is as painful to the Holy One, blessed be He, as the day the Tablets were broken; and to let you know that their declaration of, *Let us appoint a leader and go back to Egypt* (*Bamidbar* 14:4) in order to separate from [G-d], was as difficult for Him to bear as the day on which they made the golden calf.

10:12 And now, Yisrael, what does Hashem ask of You? Only that you remain in awe of Hashem your G-d, so that you will follow all His paths and love Him, serving Hashem your G-d with all your heart and with all your soul.

AND NOW, YISRAEL—Even though you have done all these [sinful things], His compassion and His love for you still endures, and despite all the sins you have committed against Him, He asks of you *only that you remain in awe of Hashem* . . .

Our Rabbis infer from this verse: Everything [that happens] is decreed in Heaven, except your fear of Heaven [which is determined by your own free will].

10:13 If you are careful to listen to My commandments which I am prescribing to you today, to love Hashem your G-d and serve Him with all your heart and soul.

IF YOU ARE CAREFUL TO LISTEN—[The literal text is *if you listen to listen,* implying:] If you listen to the old, then you will listen to the new—[if you review the material you have learned, then your previous knowledge will help you understand new information].

By the same token, the phrase, "*if forgetting you will forget,*" means: If you have begun to forget, ultimately you will forget everything [you have learned]. And so it says in *Megillas S'sarim*:

"If you abandon Me for a day, I will abandon you for two days." [A parable explains it: If two friends part, each walking away in opposite directions, at the end of one day, there will be a distance of two days separating them].

TO LOVE HASHEM YOUR G-D—Do not say, "I am learning [Torah] to become rich, . . . to be called 'rabbi,' . . . or to receive a reward." Rather, whatever you do, should be out of love [of G-d], and honor will ultimately be yours.

AND SERVE HIM WITH ALL YOUR HEART—This refers to "service of the heart," which is prayer. Prayer is called "service," as [King Darius said to Daniel,] *Your G-d whom you serve so regularly will save you* (*Daniel* 6:17). Was there service [with altar offerings] in Babylonia? Rather, [King Darius] said this because [Daniel] used to pray, as it says, *He had windows made in his upper chamber facing Yerushalayim, and three times a day he knelt down and prayed* (*Daniel* 6:5). Similarly, David said, *May my prayer be as pleasing as incense before You* (*Tehillim* 141:2).

10:16 Be careful lest your heart be tempted to go astray, and you worship other gods, bowing down to them.

TO GO ASTRAY—by turning away from the Torah. As a result you will worship other gods. As soon as a person turns away from the Torah he attaches himself to idolatry.

Similarly, David said, *For they have driven me away today, so that I cannot have a share in the portion of Hashem, and I am told, "Go and worship other gods"* (*1 Shemuel* 26:19). Did anyone [actually] tell him [to worship idols?] David meant: Since I am driven away and prevented from engaging in Torah study, I am close to worshiping other gods.

10:17 Hashem's anger will then be directed against you, and He will lock up the skies so that there will not be any rain. The land will not give forth its crops, and you will rapidly vanish from the good land that Hashem is giving you.

YOU WILL RAPIDLY VANISH—In addition to all the other sufferings, I will exile you from the land that caused you to sin.

A parable: This may be compared to a king who sent his son to attend a banquet. [Before he left,] he warned him, saying, "Don't overeat, so you will return home clean."

The son did not pay attention [to his father's warning]. Eating and drinking more than necessary, he threw up and soiled all the invited guests. Taking him by his hands and feet, they dumped him behind the palace. [So too, if Yisrael overindulges in the fruit of the Land they will be expelled from it.]

TEFILLIN

10:18 Place these words of Mine on your heart and soul. Bind them as a sign on your arm and let them be an insignia at the center of your head.

PLACE THESE WORDS OF MINE—Even after you go into exile, set yourselves apart through the performance of the mitzvos: Put on *tefillin, and* make *mezuzos,* so they should not be new to you when you return [from exile]. As it says, *Set up markers for yourself* (*Yirmeyah* 31:20), [so you will be familiar with them when you return to Eretz Yisrael].

10:19 Teach them to your children, to talk about them when you are at home, and when you walk along the road, when you lie down, and when you get up.

TO TALK ABOUT THEM—From the time your child can speak, teach him [the verse,] *Moshe commanded us the Torah* (*Devarim* 33:4), so this becomes his natural manner of speech.

Based on this verse [the Rabbis] said: When a child begins to talk, his father should speak to him in the Holy Language and teach him Torah. If he does not do so, it is as though he buries him, as it says, *[If you do this,] you and your children will long endure on the land that Hashem swore to your ancestors* (11:21), [but if not, the opposite will happen].

10:22 If you carefully safeguard and keep the entire mandate that I prescribe to you today, to love Hashem, walk in all His ways, and cling to Him.

WALK IN ALL HIS WAYS—He is compassionate, so should you be compassionate. He bestows kindnesses, so should you bestow kindnesses.

AND CLING TO HIM—Is it possible to [cling to Him]? Isn't G-d *a consuming fire* (*Devarim* 4:24)? The verse means: Cling to students [of the Torah] and to the sages, and I will consider it as though you had clung to Me.

ראה
RE'EIH

12:4 You may not do so to Hashem your G-d.

YOU MAY NOT DO SO TO HASHEM YOUR G-D—[This refers to verse 12:2 above, which states that the nations worship their gods on mountains, on hills, and under trees.] But you may not offer sacrifices to G-d in any place; rather, do this *only at the place that Hashem your G-d will choose.*

Another explanation: [This prohibition refers to the previous verse,] *You must tear down their altars . . . obliterating their names from this place,* but, *You may not do so to Hashem your G-d.* This is a negative commandment not to erase the name of Hashem, nor to uproot a stone from the Altar or from the Courtyard [of the Beis Hamikdash].

Rabbi Yishmael said: Would it enter your mind that Yisrael would demolish the sacred altars? Rather, [the verse means] that you should not act like the nations [of Canaan] causing your sins to destroy the Beis Hamikdash of your fathers.

12:23 Only be strong not to eat the blood, since the blood is [associated with] the soul, and do not ingest the soul along with the flesh.

ONLY BE STRONG NOT TO EAT THE BLOOD—The words *be strong* imply that [B'nei Yisrael] were accustomed to eating blood. That is why it was necessary to say *be strong;* these are the words of Rabbi Yehudah.

Rabbi Shimon ben Azzai says: The verse only comes to teach how ardently one must exert himself to observe the mitzvos. If regarding blood which is easy to abstain from, since no one has an appetite for it, the Torah must fortify us [against violating] its prohibition, how much more so [must we fortify ourselves] to observe other commandments [which the evil impulse tempts us to violate].

12:25 Do not eat it, in order that you and your descendants will have a good life, because you will be doing what is morally right in the eyes of Hashem.

YOU AND YOUR DESCENDANTS WILL HAVE A GOOD LIFE—We can learn [from here] how great the reward for observing the mitzvos is. If one earns a reward for himself and his descendants for abstaining from [eating] blood which people find loathsome, how much more so [does one earn a reward] for abstaining from theft and sexual immorality, for which a person has an innate propensity.

12:28 Safeguard and listen to all these things that I prescribe to you, so that you and your descendants will have a good life forever, since you will be doing that which is good and morally right in the eyes of Hashem your G-d.

SAFEGUARD—This refers to studying the *Mishnah* [which is not written down,] which one must retain inside himself so it should not be forgotten, as it says, *For it is a delight when you guard them in your stomach* (*Mishlei* 22:18).

If one studies the Mishnah, he will be able to obey and fulfill [the mitzvos]. But one who does not study the Mishnah is unable to perform [the mitzvos properly].

ALL THESE THINGS—An easy mitzvah should be as dear to you as a difficult one.

14:1 You are children of Hashem your G-d. Do not mutilate yourselves, and do not make a bald patch in the middle of your head for a dead person.

DO NOT MUTILATE YOURSELVES—Do not scratch or make an incision in your flesh over a dead person the way the Amorites do, because you are children of the Omnipresent, and are meant to be good-looking rather than disfigured and bald.

15:4 However, there will not be any poor among you, for Hashem will bless you in the land that Hashem your G-d is giving you to occupy as a heritage.

HOWEVER, THERE WILL NOT BE ANY POOR AMONG YOU—But further on it says, *The poor will never cease to exist* (15:11)! When you do the will of G-d, there are poor people among others, but not among you. When you do not do the will of G-d, there will be poor people among you.

16:11 You shall rejoice before Hashem your G-d. You [along] with your son, your daughter, your slave and your maidservant, the Levite from your settlements, the convert, the orphan, and the widow among you, in the place that Hashem your G-d shall choose to be designated in His name.

THE LEVITE, THE CONVERT, THE ORPHAN AND THE WIDOW AMONG YOU—These four of Mine correspond to your four: your son, your daughter, your slave, and your maidservant. If you make Mine happy, I will make yours happy.

———◆———

18:13 You must remain totally faithful to Hashem your G-d.

YOU MUST REMAIN TOTALLY FAITHFUL TO HASHEM YOUR G-D—
Lead your life with complete trust in Him, and depend on Him.
Do not probe into the future [by consulting fortune tellers], rather,
accept whatever happens to you with unquestioning faith. If you
do so, you will be with Him and be His portion.

20:1 When you go to battle against your enemies and see
horses, war chariots, and an army larger than yours,
do not be afraid of them, since Hashem your G-d who
brought you out of Egypt is with you.

WHEN YOU GO TO BATTLE—The Torah juxtaposes this passage
about going out to battle [next to the chapter of equitable justice]
to tell you that if you carry out just judgment, you may be confident that you will be victorious in war.

Similarly, King David says, *I have practiced justice and righteousness—you will not abandon me to my oppressors* (*Tehillim* 119:121).

20:3 He shall say to them, "Listen Yisrael! Today you are
about to wage war against your enemies. Do not be
faint-hearted, do not be afraid, do not panic, and do not break
ranks before them."

LISTEN YISRAEL—Even if the only merit you have is the recitation of the Shema, you are worthy that He shall save you.

20:8 The lower officers shall then continue speaking to the people and say, "Is there any man among you who is afraid or faint-hearted? Let him go home rather than have his cowardliness demoralize his brethren."

IS THERE ANY MAN AMONG YOU WHO IS AFRAID OR FAINT-HEART-ED—Rabbi Akiva says: [Understand these words] according to their literal meaning: He cannot stand in the closed formation of battle and look at a drawn sword.

Rabbi Yose Hagelili says: [The verse is referring to] one who is afraid [he may fall in battle] because of sins he has committed. That is why the Torah allows one who built a house, planted a vineyard, or took a wife, to return from the battlefield, covering up for those who return because of their sins. [People] will not know they are sinners, for one who sees a person returning will say, "Perhaps he has built a house, planted a vineyard, or betrothed a wife."

THE UNSOLVED MURDER

21:7 [The elders] shall speak up and say, "Our hands have not spilled this blood, and our eyes have not witnessed it."

OUR HANDS HAVE NOT SPILLED THIS BLOOD—Would it enter anyone's mind that the elders of the court are [suspect] of shedding blood? [The elders mean: "We have not even been the indirect cause of his death, for] we never saw him to let him leave without food and escort".

כי תצא
KI SEITZEI

━━━◆◆◆◆◆━━━

21:23 You may not allow his body to remain on the gallows, but you must bury it on the same day, since a person who has been hanged is a curse to Hashem. You must not let it defile the land that Hashem your G-d is giving you as a heritage.

SINCE A PERSON WHO HAS BEEN HANGED IS A CURSE TO HASHEM—
It is a disgrace for the [Divine] King, for man is created in His image, and B'nei Yisrael are His children.

A parable: This may be compared to identical twin brothers. One became an officer, and the other was arrested for robbery and hanged. Whoever saw him hanging on the gallows thought the officer was hanged.

22:7 You must first chase away the mother[14], and only then may you take the young. [If you do so] you will have it good and live long.

[IF YOU DO SO] YOU WILL HAVE IT GOOD—If the Torah rewards you for an easy mitzvah that involves no out-of-pocket expense, saying,

---

14 The Torah forbids taking an egg or chick from a nest without first sending away the mother.

You will have it good and live long, all the more so [will you be rewarded] for fulfilling difficult mitzvos [that involve monetary loss].

23:4,8,9

Neither an Ammonite nor an Moabite may enter the congregation of Hashem; even the tenth generation may not enter the congregation of Hashem forever. Do not despise an Edomite because he is your brother; do not despise an Egyptian because you sojourned in his land. Children born to them in the third generation [after becoming converts] may enter Hashem's congregation.

CHILDREN BORN TO THEM IN THE THIRD GENERATION MAY ENTER HASHEM'S CONGREGATION—Thus you learn that causing a person to sin is worse than killing him. For one who kills a person kills him in this world, [but the victim has a share in the World to Come]. But one who causes him to sin removes him from this world and from the World to Come.

Therefore, [although] Edom advanced against [Yisrael] with the sword, they are not despised [and are not prohibited from marrying a Jew forever.] Similarly, the Egyptians, who drowned [their male children,] have not become despised. But [Ammon and Mo'av] who caused [B'nei Yisrael] to sin, (see *Bamidbar* Chapter 25) have become despised [and are forbidden forever].

24:9

Remember what Hashem your G-d did to Miriam on the way when you went out of Egypt.

Remember what Hashem your G-d did to Miriam—If you wish to guard yourself from *tzaraas*, do not tell defamatory tales. Remember what happened to Miriam who was stricken with *tzaraas* for speaking [slander] against her brother [Moshe].

24:16

Fathers shall not be put to death through their sons, and sons shall not be put to death through their fathers; every man shall die for his [own] sins.

FATHERS SHALL NOT BE PUT TO DEATH THROUGH THEIR SONS—
[This means] through the testimony of their sons. You cannot say
[this means that fathers shall not be put to death] because of the sins
of their sons, since it already says, *a man shall die for his [own] sin.*

However, [*A man shall die for his own sin,* teaches, that] one
who is not yet a man, may die because of his father's sins.
[Therefore,] minors can die for the sins of their fathers by Heavenly
decree, [but not by earthly courts].

24:19 When you reap your grain harvest and forget a
sheaf in the field, you must not go back and get it.
It must be left for the foreigner, orphan and widow, so that
Hashem your G-d will bless you in all that you do.

SO THAT HASHEM YOUR G-D WILL BLESS YOU—although [the
farmer forgot the sheaf and the charitable act] was done without
intention. How much more so [will one be blessed] if he intentionally gives [charity to the needy. Based on this verse] we say
[that if] someone dropped a *sela* coin and a poor man found it and
bought food with it, [the one who lost the coin] will be blessed because of it.

25:1 When there is a dispute between men, and they go to
judgment, and a judgment is handed down, acquitting
the innocent, and convicting the guilty.

WHEN THERE IS A DISPUTE BETWEEN MEN—Ultimately, they will
have to go to court. We see from here that nothing good comes
out of a quarrel. [For example:] What caused Lot to leave the
righteous [Avraham]? Obviously, it was the quarrel.

25:17 Remember what Amalek did to you on the way
when you left Egypt.

REMEMBER WHAT AMALEK DID TO YOU—[This verse follows immediately after the prohibition against using false weights and mea-

sures, conveying this message:] If you use false weights and measures, be concerned about attack from the enemy, as it says, *A false
balance is an abomination of Hashem* (*Mishlei* 11:1), followed by,
Iniquity comes, and humiliation comes (11:2).

25:18 They encountered you on the way, when you were
tired and exhausted, and they cut off those lagging
at your rear, and they did not fear Hashem.

THEY ENCOUNTERED YOU ON THE WAY . . . Another interpretation:
[The Hebrew word for, "encountered," is *karecha* which can also
be translated as,] "cold." [Amalek] cooled you off from your boiling heat, making you lukewarm. The nations were afraid to fight
you, [just as people are afraid to touch something boiling hot.] He
[Amalek] came and began, paving the way for others.

   This may be compared to a bath that was too hot for anyone to
enter. A scoundrel came by and jumped in. Although he scalded
himself, he made it appear cold to others.

כי תבא
Ki Savo

29:3 Hashem did not give you a heart to know, eyes to see, and ears to know, until this day.

UNTIL THIS DAY—I have heard that on the day Moshe gave the Book of the Torah to the sons of Levi, as it says, *Moshe then wrote down the Torah and gave it to Levi's descendants* (31:9), all Yisrael came before Moshe, saying to him, "Moshe Rabbeinu! We, too, stood at Sinai, accepted the Torah, and it was given to us. Why do you give your tribe control over it, so that one day they may say to us, 'It was not given to you; rather, it was given to us'?"

Moshe was very happy [to hear] this. Therefore, he said, *Today you have become a nation to Hashem your G-d* (27:9). [Implying,] today I realize that you are attached to the Omnipresent and desire Him.

נצבים

NITZAVIM

———◆———

29:12 In order to establish you today as His nation, so that He will be a G-d to you, just as He promised you, and as He swore to your ancestors, Avraham, Yitzchak, and Yaakov.

SO THAT HE WILL BE A G-D TO YOU—Speaking about you, He promised your forefathers not to exchange their descendants for another nation. For this reason He binds you with these oaths not to provoke His anger, inasmuch as He cannot separate Himself from you.

Up to this point I have explained the text according to the literal sense of the chapter. However, an Aggadic explanation is as follows:

Why does the portion of "*You are standing today*" follow immediately after the curses [in *parashas Ki Savo*]? When Yisrael heard these ninety-eight curses, in addition to the forty-nine curses in *Toras Kohanim*[15], their faces turned pale [with fright], and they exclaimed, "Who can possibly survive these [curses]?"

[Therefore,] Moshe reassured them, saying, *You are standing today,* [implying,] although you have angered G-d repeatedly, He has not wiped you out, rather you are still alive and well before Him.

TODAY—Like the day which reappears forever. [Although] it turns dark [at night] it shines again [in the morning]. So too, He has given you [periods of] light [and good fortune] and will once again make you shine. The curses and sufferings sustain you and keep you standing before Him.

30:3 Hashem your G-d will bring back your captivity and have mercy on you. Hashem your G-d will return and gather you from among all the nations where He scattered you.

HASHEM YOUR G-D WILL BRING BACK YOUR CAPTIVITY—[The Hebrew term for *will bring back* used here is *veshav* which literally means, "He will come back."] The verse should have said *veheishiv* which means *He will bring back*. Our Rabbis learned from this—if one may say this [of Hashem]—that the *Shechinah* dwells with Yisrael in the plight of their exile. And when [Yisrael] is redeemed, [G-d] ascribes redemption to Himself, namely, that He returns [from exile] along with [Yisrael].

Another interpretation: The day of the ingathering of the exiles is so great, and it will come about with so much difficulty, that it is as though [G-d] Himself must actually hold each and every person with His hand, taking him out from his place [in the exile], as it says, *You shall be picked up, one by one, O B'nei Yisrael* (*Yeshayah* 27:12).

We find the same expression used in connection with the gathering of the exiles of other nations, as, *I will return the captivity of Egypt* (*Yechezkel* 29:4).

30:12 [The Torah] is not in heaven, so [that you should] say, "Who shall go up to heaven and bring it to us so that we can hear it and keep it?"

[THE TORAH] IS NOT IN HEAVEN—[This is a special favor, for] if [the Torah] were in heaven we would have to go up after it to learn it [for the Torah is our life].

30:19 I call heaven and earth as witnesses against you! Before you I have placed life and death, the blessing and the curse. You must choose life, so that you and your descendants will survive.

I CALL HEAVEN AND EARTH AS WITNESSES AGAINST YOU!—For they exist forever. And when bad things will happen to you, they will testify that I have warned you about all this.

Another explanation: *I call heaven and earth as witnesses against you*—The Holy One, blessed be He, said to Yisrael, "Look! I have created the heavens to serve you. Did they ever change their nature? Has the sphere of the sun ever failed to rise in the east, and shine on the whole world, as it says, *The sun rises and the sun sets* (*Koheles* 1:5)? Look at the earth which I created to serve you. Did it ever change its nature? Did you ever sow seeds in the earth that did not sprout? Did you sow wheat, and [the earth] produced barley?"

[The sun and the earth] were made neither for reward nor loss. If they are worthy, [and follow the laws of nature,] they do not receive reward, and if they disobey, they do not receive punishment, yet they never veer from the laws of nature. How much more so should you, who if you are worthy will receive reward, and if you sin you will receive punishment, [not veer from the laws of the Torah].

YOU MUST CHOOSE LIFE—I instruct you to choose the portion of life. This is similar to one who says to his son, "Choose for yourself a good portion in my property," directing him to the best portion, and telling him, "Pick this for yourself."

Concerning this it says, *Hashem is my allotted share and my cup. You guide my portion* (*Tehillim* 16:5). You placed my hand on the good portion, saying, "Choose this for yourself!"

וילך

VA'YELECH

———————————

31:21 When they will beset with many evils and troubles, this song shall declare for them as a witness, since it will not be forgotten by their descendants. Because I know their [evil] impulse through what they are doing today, even before I have brought them to the land that I promised.

SINCE IT WILL NOT BE FORGOTTEN BY THEIR DESCENDANTS—[*This song* refers to the Torah, and] this verse contains a promise to Yisrael that the Torah will never be entirely forgotten by their descendants.

32:2 My lesson shall fall like rain, my saying shall drip down like the dew—like a stormy wind on the herb, like a shower on the grass.

MY LESSON SHALL FALL LIKE RAIN—The Torah that I gave to Yisrael gives life to the world, just as the heavens drip down life-giving dew and rain to the world.

LIKE A STORMY WIND ON THE HERB—Just as these winds fortify the plants, promoting their growth, so do the words of Torah strengthen and elevate [the spiritual stature] of those who study them.

32:4 The deeds of the Rock are perfect, for all His ways are just. He is a faithful G-d and never unfair, righteous and moral is He.

THE DEEDS OF THE ROCK ARE PERFECT—Although He is strong, [able to destroy the world in an instant,] He does not bring punishment on those who transgress His will in a torrent [of anger,] but rather with [deliberate] judgment, because *His deeds are perfect.*

HE IS A FAITHFUL G-D—Faithful to pay the righteous for their righteousness in the World to Come. Although He delays their reward,

ultimately He will be faithful to His word [granting them a boun-
tiful share in the World to Come].

AND NEVER UNFAIR—[He is never unfair] even to the wicked, re-
warding them in this world for their [few] righteous deeds.

RIGHTEOUS AND MORAL IS HE—All acknowledge that He judged
them with righteousness, and [His punishment for their offenses]
is fitting and proper.

32:8 When the Most High gave nations their heritage and
split up the sons of man, He set up the borders of nations according to the number of B'nei Yisrael.

WHEN THE MOST HIGH GAVE NATIONS THEIR HERITAGE—When
the Holy One, blessed be He, apportioned the fate they deserved
to those who angered Him, He flooded and drowned them.

AND SPLIT UP THE SONS OF MAN—He split up the generation of the
Dispersion. Though He had the power to remove them from the
world, He did not do so, rather, *He set up the borders of nations*—
keeping them alive and not destroying them.

ACCORDING TO THE NUMBER OF B'NEI YISRAEL—[He did not destroy them] because of the number of B'nei Yisrael who were destined to be born from the children of Shem.

HE SET UP THE BORDERS OF NATIONS—Corresponding to the
seventy children of Yisrael who went down to Egypt, [He made]
seventy nations, who speak seventy [different] languages.

32:9 But His own Nation remained Hashem's portion,
Yaakov the measuring rope of His heritage.

BUT HIS OWN NATION REMAINED HASHEM'S PORTION—Why [did
G-d do] all this, [sparing the sinful generation of the Dispersion]?

Because His portion was contained in them and was destined to come forth [from them]. Who is G-d's portion? His people. And who is His people? *Yaakov, the measuring rope of His heritage.*

YAAKOV THE MEASURING ROPE OF HIS HERITAGE—He is the third Patriarch, thus endowed with a threefold merit—the merit of his grandfather, the merit of his father, and his own merit. These three are like a rope made up of three strands. Only Yaakov and his sons became G-d's heritage; excluding Yishmael, the son of Avraham, and Eisav, the son of Yitzchak.

PUNISHMENT FOR CRIMES AGAINST YISRAEL

32:42 I will make My arrows drunk with blood, My sword consuming flesh. The enemy's first punishment will be the blood of the slain and wounded.

THE ENEMY'S FIRST PUNISHMENT—[will be] for his crime of making the first breach [in Yisrael]. For when the Holy One, blessed be He, punishes the nations [for the atrocities they have committed against Yisrael,] He keeps in mind their own sin and the sins of their ancestors, going back to the first breach they made against Yisrael.

32:43 Let the nations sing praise to His people, for He will avenge His servants' blood. He will bring vengeance on His foes, and appease His land and His people.

LET THE NATIONS SING PRAISE TO HIS PEOPLE—At that time [when I take revenge on Yisrael's enemies,] the nations will praise Yisrael, saying, "How praiseworthy is this nation! They remained committed to the Holy One, blessed be He, throughout all the hardships they endured. They did not forsake Him, but recognized His

---

15 *Vayikra* 26:14-44

goodness and His praiseworthy [attributes, even in their darkest hour]."

32:46 He said to them, "Pay close attention to all the words through which I warn you today, so that you will be able to instruct your children to keep all the words of this Torah carefully."

PAY CLOSE ATTENTION—A person must focus his eyes, ears, and heart on the words of the Torah. Indeed it says, *Son of man, see with your eyes, and listen with your ears, and apply your heart to all that I show you* [namely, the plan of the Beis Hamikdash] (*Yechezkel* 40:4,5).

We can draw a logical conclusion from this. If one must concentrate his eyes, ears, and heart to understand the [tangible] plan of the Beis Hamikdash which can be seen with the eyes, and which is measured with a measuring rod, how much more so must he [concentrate] to understand the words of the Torah which are compared to "mountains hanging by a hair."

32:47 It, [the Torah,] is not an empty teaching for you. It is your life, and with it you will long endure on the land which you are crossing the Yardein to occupy.

IT IS NOT AN EMPTY TEACHING FOR YOU—You are not toiling in vain. A great reward accompanies it—it is your life.

Another explanation: If you expound on any seemingly superfluous word in the Torah, it will bring a reward.

Proof of this can be had from the words of our Rabbis: It says, *Timna was the sister of [the chieftain] Lotan* (*Bereishis* 36:22), and it says, *Timna was a concubine of Elifaz, son of Eisav* (36:32). [Why would Timna, a chieftain's sister become a concubine?] Because Timna said, ["Although I am a chieftain's sister,] I am not worthy to be the wife [of Avraham's grandson Elifaz]. I wish I were [at least] his concubine."

And why does the Torah tell us this [seemingly trivial] matter?

To tell us that Avraham was so highly esteemed that rulers and kings were eager to attach themselves to him [by marrying into his family].

32:48 Hashem spoke to Moshe at the very height of that day saying.

AT THE VERY HEIGHT OF THAT DAY—In three places [in the Torah] the expression, *on the very height of that day* is used.

In connection with Noach it says, *On the very height of that day Noach came into the ark* (*Bereishis* 7:1), meaning, "at high noon." The people of his generation said, "[We swear] by such and such [idol], that if we notice Noach [preparing to enter the ark,] we won't permit him to enter the ark. Not only that, we will take sledgehammers and axes and wreck the ark." Therefore the Holy One, blessed be He, said, "You'll see, I will bring him into [the ark] at high noon. Whoever has the power to stop him, let him come and stop him!"

Regarding Egypt it says, *On the very height of that day, Hashem took B'nei Yisrael out of Egypt* (*Shemos* 12:11). The Egyptians said, "[We swear] by such and such [idol] that if we notice them [preparing to leave,] we won't let them go. Not only that, we will take swords and other weapons and kill them."

Said the Holy One, blessed be He, "I will take them out at noon. If anyone has the power to stand in the way, let him come and stand in the way."

Here too, at the death of Moshe, it says, *At the very height of that day.* B'nei Yisrael said, "We swear that if we notice Moshe about to die, we won't let him go. [This is] the man who took us out of Egypt, split the sea for us, brought down the *manna* for us, made the quail fly toward us, caused [the water of] the well to rise for us, and gave us the Torah. We won't let go of him!"

The Holy One, blessed be He, replied, "I will make him enter [the mountain where he will die] *at the very height of that day.*

32:51 This,[16] because you broke faith with me in the midst of B'nei Yisrael in the Waters of Dispute at Kadeish in the Tzin Desert, and because you did not sanctify Me among B'nei Yisrael.

BECAUSE YOU DID NOT SANCTIFY ME AMONG B'NEI YISRAEL—You caused that I not be sanctified, when I said to you [and Aharon,] "Speak to the rock," (*Bamidbar* 20:8). They struck it instead, and had to strike it twice. Had they spoken to it so it gave water without being struck, the Name of Heaven would have been sanctified, for Yisrael would have said, "If this rock which can expect neither reward nor punishment—if it is worthy [and fulfills G-d's command] it receives no reward, and if it transgresses it is not punished—fulfills the commandments of its Creator, how much more so should we [who receive reward and punishment,] fulfill His commands.

---

16 Moshe and Aharon were told they would die because of the sin of striking the rock.

וזאת הברכה
VEZOS HABERACHAH

———◆———

33:3 Although there is love of nations, all Your holy ones are in Your hand. [They deserve this,] for they placed themselves beneath Your footsteps and bear Your utterances.

ALL YOUR HOLY ONES ARE IN YOUR HAND—The souls of the righteous are hidden away with Him, as it says, *May the soul of my master be bound up in the bond of life with Hashem your G-d* (1 *Shemuel* 25:29).

FOR THEY PLACED THEMSELVES BENEATH YOUR FEET—They are worthy of [having their souls stored with You,] for they placed themselves [at Your feet] underneath the mountain of Sinai.

Another explanation [of this passage:]
ALTHOUGH THERE IS LOVE OF NATIONS—Even when You show love to the nations of the world, smiling at them, and delivering Yisrael into their power, *all Your holy ones are in Your hand*—all Yisrael's righteous and good people remain close to You, not moving away from You, and You guard them.

FOR THEY PLACED THEMSELVES BENEATH YOUR FEET—They came together and gathered beneath Your shadow.

HE WOULD BEAR YOUR UTTERANCES—[B'nei Yisrael] joyfully accepted upon themselves Your decrees and edicts.

33:5 [Hashem] was King in Yeshurun when the nation's leaders gather together, [and] the tribes of Yisrael are united.

WHEN THE NATION'S LEADERS GATHER TOGETHER—When they gather together in a single group in peace, He is their King, but not when there is strife among them.

33:11 May Hashem bless his army[17] and favor the work of his hands. May he smash the loins of those who rise up against him, so that his enemies rise no more.

MAY HE SMASH THE LOINS OF THOSE WHO RISE UP AGAINST HIM— [Moshe] foresaw that [Mattisyahu, the] Chashmona'i and his sons were destined to wage war against the Greeks. [Therefore,] he prayed for them, because they were few [in number]—the twelve sons of [Mattisyahu the] Chashmona'i and Elazar—against tens of thousands of them. Therefore it says, *May Hashem bless his army and favor the work of his hand*.

33:19 They[18] shall assemble nations to the mountains, and there they shall offer righteous sacrifice. They will be nourished by the bounty of the sea and by what is hidden in the secret treasures of the sand.

THEY SHALL ASSEMBLE NATIONS TO THE MOUNTAINS—Through the commercial ties of Zevulun, the merchants of the nations of the world came to his region which is situated on the [Mediterranean] coast. They said, "Since we have exerted ourselves to get here, let's

---

17 The army of the tribe of Levi.
18 The tribe of Zevulun.

go up Yerushalayim and examine the religion of this [Jewish] nation and see their way of life.

When they [come to Yerushalayim] and see all Jews worshiping one G-d and eating the same [kosher] food [they are amazed,] because the god of one [idolatrous nations] is not like the god of another, and the food of one nation is not as the food of another. They will say, *There is no nation as upright as this one,* and they will convert to Judaism, as it says, *There [in Yerushalayim] they will slaughter offerings of righteous [converts].*

34:8 B'nei Yisrael mourned Moshe on the plains of Moav for thirty days.

B'NEI YISRAEL—[Only] the men [mourned him.] By contrast, it says about Aharon, *The entire House of Yisrael mourned him* (*Bamidbar* 20:20)—both the men and the women. [He was loved by all,] because he pursued peace, making peace between man and his fellow man and between husband and wife.

GLOSSARY

ADAM HARISHON - Adam the first man
AGGADAH - Homiletic discourses
AHARON - Aaron
AVRAHAM - Abraham
BAMIDBAR - The Book of Numbers
BEIS HAMIKDASH - Holy Temple
BEN - Son of
BEREISHIS - The Book of Genesis
BILAM - Ballam
B'NEI YISRAEL - Children of Israel
CHUPPAH - Canopy for marriage ceremony
DEVARIM - The Book of Deuteronomy
DIVREI HAYAMIM - The Book of Chronicles
EISAV - Esau
ELIYAHU - Elijah
ELOHIM - God
ERETZ YISRAEL - The Land of Israel
GAN EDEN - The garden of Eden
HASHEM - God
KAREIS - Punishment of premature death
KOHEIN GADOL - High Priest
KOHEIN pl. *KOHANIM* -Priests, descendants of Aaron
KOHELES - Ecclesiastes
KORBAN - Sacrifice
LASHON HORA - Gossip
LAVAN - Laban
LEVI'IM, LEVITE - From the tribe of Levi
MELACHIM - The Book of Kings
Metzora - One afflicted with Tzaraas
MEZUZAH PL. MEZUZOS - Parchment scrolls containing the Shema
    that is placed on the doorpost.
MIDRASH - Homelitic discourse

121

MISHKAN - The Tabernacle

MISHLEI - Proverbs

MISHNAH pl. *MISHNAYOS* - Compilation of the oral tradition; it also
refers to one paragraph of this compilation.

MITZVAH pl. *MITZVOS* - Commandment

NAZIR, NAZIRITE - One who makes a vow to abstain from wine and
from contact with the dead

NOACH - Noah

ONKELOS - A convert who wrote an Aramaic translation of the Torah

PARASHAS - The portion [of the Torah]

PESACH - Passover

RUACH HAKODESH - Divine inspiration

SANHEDRIN - Jewish High Court

SHABBOS - The day of rest - Saturday

SHACHARIS - The morning prayer

SHAVUOS - Festival of Weeks

SHECHINA - Divine Presence

SHELOMOH - Solomon

SHEMA - The portion of the Torah containing the declaration of
Hashem's unity that we are required to recite twice daily.

SHMITTAH - The sabbatical year when work in the field is prohibited

SHEMOS - The Book of Exodus

SHEMUEL - The Book of Samuel

SHOFTIM - The Book of Judges

SUKKOS - Festival of Tabernacles

TALLIS - Prayer Shawl

TANACH - Scriptures

TEFILLIN - Phylacteries

TEHILLIM - Psalms

TESHUVAH - Repentance

TZADDIK pl. *TZADDIKIM* - Pious Person

TZARAAS - Leprosy

TZITZIS - Fringes worn on a four cornered garment

URIM V'TUMIM - Script of the Divine Name placed in the fold of the
Kohein Gadol's breastplate.

VAYIKRA - The Book of Leviticus

YAAKOV - Jacob

YECHEZKEL - Ezekiel

YEHOSHUA - Joshua

YERUSHALAYIM - Jerusalem

YESHAYAH - Isaiah

YIRMEYAH - Jeremiah

YISRAEL - Israel

YITZCHOCK - Isaac